"This book will be of interest to anyone with an interest in the history of childbirth in America and wants to understand the roots of midwifery in caring for women and families"
Ira Kantrowitz-Gordon, PhD, CNM, ARNP
Director, Graduate Nurse-Midwifery Education Program
University of Washington, School of Nursing; Seattle, WA

"Susan pulls the reader back in time, to experience the hardships, challenges, joys and courage of birthing during the early 1900's. As an obstetrical nurse, I was fascinated by the book and am reading it a second time."
Margene Chantry, BSN, RN, L & D Nurse
Mother of 18, Washington

"I found the birth stories to be absolutely captivating and perfectly done with descriptions of the conditions and not the current medical names. Alice's wisdom in caring for women in labor was timeless. She was caring and non-judgmental. I wish I could have known her."
Colonel Richard Jackson M.D. OBGYN
US Army San Antonio, TX

"This book is an excellent teaching tool, filled with complex birth stories, waiting to be analyzed and discussed by midwifery and medical/obstetric students alike."
Sara S. Vranes, editor, Lactation Specialist, Doula
Apprentice Midwife – Midwives College of UT

"This book celebrates the sanctity of every human life told through the story of a remarkable family! Within the context of a young Seattle, life and death issues which still face the unborn and newly born are confronted: abortion, abuse, neglect, and abandonment."
Mark Ralston M.D. MPH Pediatrician
Oak Harbor, Whidbey Island WA

"Excellent combination of story telling and history of obstetrical care in the early 1900's."
Deb Castile MN, RNc, Perinatal CNS, NE
Perinatal Safety Program Manager, Oregon

"This book eloquently captures the joys, fears, and intensity of childbirth that only one who has the privilege of participating in it on a daily basis can convey. Alice was a true pioneer. As practitioners of her craft we are forever indebted to her courage and sacrifice."
Aron Schuftan MD OBGYN Redwood City, CA

"Susan takes the reader on a journey through poignant accounts of women's birth experiences in our country's 'wild' West. This book is a 'must read' for all, especially those of us who practice the art and science of nursing."
~Katherine O'Connell MN, RN Perinatal CNS
University of Washington Medical Center, Seattle, WA

Alice Ada Wood Ellis

Seattle Pioneer Midwife

Alice Ada Wood Ellis

Midwife, Nurse & Mother to All

As told by her great-granddaughter
SUSAN E. FLEMING

Seattle Pioneer Midwife
Alice Ada Wood Ellis
Midwife, Nurse & Mother to All

Second edition March 17, 2014
Susan E. Fleming PhD, Perinatal CNS

Edited by
Dana Rose Fleming
Edward Fleming
Contributors
Annika Fleming
Monika Fleming
Harrison Fleming

Technical Adviser
Edward Oscar Fleming, CRNA

Library of Congress
Published in the United States of America
ISBN: 1494763524
ISBN-13: 978-1494763527

DEDICATION

This book is dedicated to mothers and to everyone who has or will compassionately support a woman-with-child to accomplish the great feat and miracle of birthing. Furthermore, it is dedicated to all unclaimed children. May they find a place to call home and be loved. The hope is that this book and Alice's example will encourage everyone to see beyond the obvious and take part in discovering and creating the future.

And special tribute to:

Dr. Rosemary Casey, DO, OBGYN
Becky RN & Dr. Rich Jackson, MD, OBGYN
Alex & Kathy Capiro, RN

May this book be an expression of gratitude for their
contribution to the well-being
of women and children and
for enduring such temporal hardships.

"When we can no longer change the situation, we are challenged to change ourselves."
~Viktor Frankl

Alice Ada Wood Ellis

TABLE OF CONTENTS

* Time Frame

Preface

As a tribute to Alice, I have made every attempt to recount the stories carefully that has been passed down from generation to generation. Nevertheless, stories change as decades pass. All of the birthing stories are based on actual births from Alice's time as passed down from my grandmother Marie to me, my Aunt Mary, my father Bill or births that I have experienced as my own or ones that I attended as a Labor and Delivery nurse. I believe that the dates, based on official records and written accounts, are accurate.

The book integrates historical figures and data (from the US Census; newspapers; family genealogy; city, state, and national libraries; and historical websites). I've added a few fictional stories and characters to supplement this story in an attempt to capture the lifestyle of a pioneer midwife, nurse, and caretaker of children in the early 1900s in Seattle, Washington.

At times, I use the medical terminology of the era in describing the birth stories. Students can apply current medical terminology to the details and descriptions of each case. This book may be used in conjunction with current textbooks as a means to compare and contrast current birthing practices with those of one hundred years ago.

The material in this book is intended to be informational and historical only. **It is not intended to be used as medical advice** during pregnancy, birthing, postpartum or newborn care. Some of the procedures described in this book may be harmful to mother or baby. Mothers-to-be are advised to contact their own health professionals during pregnancy and birthing.

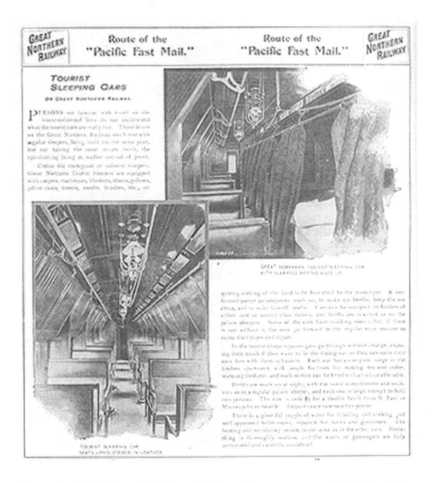

Illustration 1. A Great Northern Railway flyer, courtesy of Ted Doyle.[1]

"Work, hard work, intelligent work, and then more work."
~James Hill, railroad entrepreneur

1

1900~Taking the Train West

Great Northern Railway

Alice Ada Wood Ellis was thirty-two years old and had just boarded a locomotive steam train, the Great Northern Flyer, for the final leg of a grueling journey.[1] As the train pulled out of the Saint Paul, Minnesota, train depot at ten o'clock in the morning, the whistle blew. It could have been blowing for Alice: her life had changed and she was moving west.

She was ready. She had started her journey in Milwaukee and then transferred to a commuter train, The Milwaukee Road.[1-4] Her intention was to reach Seattle, Washington, in fewer than sixty hours.

Snow had fallen overnight and glistened in the morning sun. The Christmas season of 1900 had arrived. The train was filled with passengers traveling west to reunite with their families over the holiday season.

Alice was dressed for the occasion. She wore a gray walking skirt that covered her buttoned-up boots and a dark-gray wool jacket. Her hair was twisted into a bun adorned with a fancy, black, metal comb. Alice was driven to make a better life for herself and her two young daughters. Myrtle was two and a half years old and Marie was a six-month-old baby; they were accompanying Alice on this journey. Her supportive mother, Clara Wood, was by her side and had made this expedition possible.

Life is change.

Alice's sixty-four-year-old father, Pierson E. Wood, had forged ahead six months earlier. A born explorer, Pierson had traveled to Seattle in June aboard a modern locomotive steam train, The Northwest Limited, to look for work and secure a temporary residence for his family. His son Eddie and his oldest daughter Beulah accompanied him on this remarkable exploration. This train had electricity and all of the bells and whistles to make traveling a pleasure.[3, 5] Unfortunately, this train did not have a winter service, so it was unavailable for Clara,

Alice, and the girls to take when they left in December.

Clara had spoken with a few of her lady friends who had recently emigrated from Norway, and they advised her to place a hump on top of the trunk to insure it would be the last trunk to be loaded on the train and therefore more protected. More importantly, it would be the first trunk to be unloaded when she arrived in Seattle. Clara had instructed Pierson to make the trunk to these specifications.

Illustration 2. Humpback trunk, 1895, courtesy of www.legacytrunks.com.

Only three years earlier, on July 17, 1897, the people of Seattle had rushed down to the waterfront to welcome the *Portland*, a steamship loaded with two tons of gold and other precious metals. This was the first delivery of metals that had been mined from the banks of the Klondike River, located in the most northwestern part of Canada, the Yukon.[6, 7] People with many different trades were needed to support the growing population of Seattle. Alice, Pierson, and the family were answering the call.

James J. Hill, an empire builder, had begun the enormous undertaking of connecting the Midwest to Seattle.[2, 3] Eastern railroad tycoons, such as Cornelius Vanderbilt, built their railroads to support the local populations.[2, 3] But in the vast, unpopulated, Wild West, Hill had to build the local populations to support his railways.[2] He achieved this by providing small towns with the financial resources to build schools and productive communities along the train routes.[2]

One of Hill's legendary accomplishments was boring a two-and-a-half-mile tunnel through the North Cascades, a mountain range in western Washington. This venture shaved off eight and a half miles of dangerous switchbacks on the route through Stevens Pass.[2,]

Even without two very young children, travel by steam train had its challenges. The train made frequent water stops, disrupting even the soundest sleeper. Worse, rumors abounded that Butch Cassidy and his Wild Bunch gang were heading north to cash in on Klondike gold-rush riches! The predictable water stops made train robbery an efficient endeavor. Alice and Clara were careful to take necessary precautions against robberies, keeping themselves on guard during this journey.

During the latter part of the nineteenth century in the United States, train robbery was a common occurrence—especially in the isolated, unpopulated West. This resulted in financial trepidation for all parties concerned, including the passengers, the train companies, the developers of western towns, the banks, and the law. Train companies took a defensive stance by employing detectives and law agencies to combat this costly occurrence, which was undermining passenger confidence, particularly in the West.[8-11]

Butch Cassidy's Wild Bunch gang was organized in 1896 drawing expert outlaws from across the West.[9] They were known for their felonious expertise in the fields of train, bank, and mine-payroll robbery.

Between 1896 and 1900, they went on a train-robbing rampage in Idaho, Wyoming, and New Mexico, and stole a large payroll in Utah.[8-11] They used clever tactics such as cutting telegraph lines so that lawmen could not be informed of their deeds.[10]

Illustration 3. Photo of Butch Cassidy, (Library of Congress.)

The railroads hired the Pinkerton National Detective Agency in the late 1890s to eliminate this notorious gang. The news got out, leading Butch and the Sundance Kid to formulate an escape plan via New York to Argentina, a place where they could purchase land and become respectable ranchers—at least, to start. To finance this endeavor, they robbed a bank in Winnemucca, Nevada, in September 1900.[9] This was just three months prior to Alice's train ride west. The Wild Bunch's final train robbery targeted a Great Northern train in Montana on July 3, 1901. They took in more than $60,000.[11] This robbery was just six months after Alice, Clara, and the girls traveled west through Montana.

Life is sinister.

Train robberies were costly and quite frightening for families traveling west, many of whom had sold their homes and farms to finance their travel and relocation. This is exactly what Alice's family had done.

ONE WAS 'BUTCH' CASSIDY
Seen Going North Prior to G.N. Train Robbery

Special Dispatch to the Standard. Deer Lodge, July 18–Sheriff Conley of Deer Lodge County was here today and with a conversation with a Standard reporter he said that he had it on good authority that one of the men who robbed the Great Northern train near Wagner on July 3 was 'Butch' Cassidy, a notorious robber and horse thief. Mr. Conley says that Will Savage of Miles City was informed by a man living on the Yellowstone that three men crossed that stream some days prior to the Great Northern hold-up going northward. One of them was Longabaugh, already...

Illustration 4. Text from an article in the *Anaconda Standard*, Deer Lodge, Montana, July 3, 1901. GenologyBank.com

Pierson was a journeyman stonecutter and member of Stone Couters (sic) Association.[5] In 1880, he had moved his family from Madison, Wisconsin, to Milwaukee, where they lived for twenty years.[5]

During the spring of 1900, the Woods sold their home and combined the proceeds with a small sum of savings to finance their relocation to Seattle. The thought of losing their life savings to these train robbers was a sobering one. Pierson and his family carefully considered safety as they ventured west. Clara ingeniously sewed some of their money between bundles of diapers wrapped with pink ribbons.

The train had advertised sleepers. However, their meager budget only financed an open bay separated by curtains.[1] It was not quite the privacy they had hoped for. They had carefully brought a mix of diapers—a few to throw away, the pink-ribboned bundles not to be opened, and a few to wash at nighttime. They hung the diapers to dry over their beds, behind the privacy curtains, where they would not be noticed. Traveling with a toddler and a baby was demanding. In addition, with the train robbery scare, they were careful not to leave their belongings unguarded.

Illustration 5. Sundance Kid and Etta Place photographed in New York just prior to their departure for South America in 1901. (Library of Congress.)

To Alice and Clara's astonishment, the little girls were delightfully calm during the train journey. Whether it was the rhythmic motion of the train, the whistle blows, or the sense that they, too, could contribute to the tranquility of this endeavor will never be known. But they were serene.

As the oil lamps dimmed, Grandma Clara said a few extra prayers that night.

Early Monday morning, they all awoke. They had brought several wool blankets to keep themselves warm as they traveled on the train. Neither of the women wanted to be the first to leave her warm cocoon and face the coolness of morning. Regardless, Myrtle and Marie were ready to get up.

Alice gazed out the icy cold window and saw a white blanket of snow covering the Montana landscape. She had never seen skies so big.

Life is picturesque.

Illustration 5. An ad for the Great Northern Flyer, courtesy of Ted Doyle.[1]

Alice wondered where the grand mountains she had read about were. They were traveling through the badlands of Montana. Are we on the moon? She said to herself, chuckling.

Pierson had described the majestic volcanic mountains near Seattle in a telegraph to his wife, Clara, and Alice. In one more day, she would see them.

Clara and Alice took turns going to the ladies' room to tend to themselves while the other cared for the little girls.

These courageous women, who were traveling without a man, intrigued the other passengers. The passengers frequently stopped by to chat about the adventure of relocating out West.

Alice, Clara, and the little girls ventured to the dining car, where they found tables covered with beautiful, white-linen tablecloths and set with bone china and silver napkin rings. They made a joint decision to eat breakfast daily in the dining car, since it was the lowest-priced meal of the day. They had brought extra food to cover lunch and dinner.

Within the hour, just after the noon, they would be arriving in Havre, Montana. The train would be making a stop, and they could get out and walk. The train provided daily mail service between Seattle and Saint Paul, a revolutionary means of transcontinental communication.[1]

As Monday evening drew to a close, Clara and the girls fell asleep. Alice decided to take a walk down to the library car.

Alice was tall, and her large eyes were deeply set. She had beautiful, soft, curly, brown hair that she rolled neatly into a bun. Her smile was warm and welcoming.

In America during the early 1900s, a woman's clothing was an expression of her status. It was evident by Alice's dress that she came from a meager background. But her clothing could not reveal her sensible demeanor and vigor. She was young and eager to start a new life. She had been given a second chance. With the love of her parents and very young daughters, she could accomplish anything she desired.

Illustration 7. Postcard of Spokane train station in 1902, courtesy of Ted Doyle.[1]

Alice agreed with her parents that the story would be that she was a widow. Most people asked too many questions, and this pretense would end unwelcome inquiries about her life.

How had her life changed so quickly? What did Seattle hold for her? How would she succeed financially and support her young family as a single mother? Those were questions she contemplated as she sat in solitude in the back of the library car. Tomorrow, her new life would begin.

The next morning, Tuesday, December 25, 1900, was Christmas Day. Alice and Clara rose early with toddler Myrtle and baby Marie and had breakfast. The train would be stopping in Spokane, and they were ready to get out and walk a bit.

They would be in Seattle that very night!

After breakfast, they conversed with other passengers. The man sitting across from Clara looked like a silver miner; his hands and his apparel were tarnished and worn. He told Clara that he was eagerly heading home to Spokane. He asked, "So where are you folks from?"

Alice responded, "Milwaukee."

At the same time Clara answered, "Madison. Well, we're originally from Madison."

The aging silver miner rambled, "Aw, yep, we had a young man from Madison living in Spokane. His name were Webster. Yep, I believe George Webster was his name. Have you heard of him?"

Alice shook her head.

Clara mentioned, "I knew some Websters in Madison; not sure if this man would be the same Webster."

Then the silver miner boldly exclaimed, "They sent him on a Texas cake walk, you know. They hung him earlier this year, a public hanging, right in front of the Spokane Courthouse. It was fer murder." [12, 13]

Alice and Clara remained silent.

The silver miner continued, "Yep, apparently Webster was jest twenty-five years old. Had a good reputation—hard worker. But one night, he drank too much alcohol and shot and killed a woman—mother of three young uns. Yep. Alcohol can lead a good man wrong. I thought they were gonna send him to the Big Pasture. They say he had no family. His parents died when he was a youngster. Let's jest say he was raised by bars, saloons, and wild women. Sad story."

Alice and Clara were silent. They were not aware that people were still being hanged for doing wrong—in public and for viewing, no less. They were about to join the Wild West.

Illustration 8. Invitation to the hanging of murderer George Webster. He was actually hanged in Spokane on March 30, 1900. Over 6,000 people petitioned to save his life. Notice the noose used as a frame for the invitation. In 1901, Washington changed the law so that all executions would be conducted inside the penitentiary. Webster's hanging was the third public hanging in Spokane in a decade. The State of Washington conducted its last hanging on May 27, 1994.[12, 13] Permission granted from Spokesman Review.

Illustration 9. Anatomy Class at the Milwaukee County Training School of Nursing. Reprinted with the permission from the Milwaukee School of Engineering School of Nursing.

"The only person you are destined to become is the person you decide to be."
~Ralph Waldo Emerson

2

1895~Attending School

Milwaukee County Training School of Nursing

In the latter part of the nineteenth century, there was a concerted effort in the United States to formally train and instruct nurses. Initially, hospital-based diploma programs took on this challenge. The goal was to provide classroom as well as apprentice learning environments, where more experienced nurses trained the student nurses. The students were given room and board, and a small stipend for their services. It was a win-win for all, especially for the hospitals. Milwaukee County Hospital joined the program in the 1880s, establishing a nursing school based on the Bellevue System or model.[14]

Bellevue Hospital in New York City integrated the teaching of Florence Nightingale's ideas, which were developed in nursing schools and hospitals such as Saint Thomas's Hospital in London.[14, 15] This became known as the Bellevue model. Dr. Connell, the Milwaukee County Hospital superintendent, and his wife Dr. Anna Connell, founded and developed the Milwaukee County Training School of Nursing.[14]

Hospitals were rapidly growing from a mere 178 in 1872 to a substantial increase of over 4,000 hospitals by 1910. Most of them stemmed from systems such as religious based ones, like Sisters of Providence; or non-denominational, primarily Protestant; public hospitals, from almshouses; marine hospitals, managed by the federal government; private hospitals, managed by doctors; and illness based hospitals, such as orthopedics or polio. [15]

The Milwaukee County Training School of Nursing was officially established in 1888, and the first class of thirteen students graduated in 1889.[14] Quickly, the school decided to add an additional year of instruction to create a two-year program. By 1903, the program had been extended to three years. A three-month obstetric clinical rotation was added in 1907, followed by a pediatric clinical rotation.[14]

Illustration 10. Milwaukee County Training School of Nursing Class of 1892, reprinted with the permission from the Milwaukee School of Engineering School of Nursing.

Prior to the 1870s, nursing was seen as an unskilled trade. Essentially, there were no trained nurses in American hospitals.[15] Many nurses employed in hospitals came from the ranks of the working poor, or from penitentiaries or almshouses—homes for the indigent.[15]

In 1872, the women of New York's State Charities Aid Association formed a committee and decided to monitor the conditions of public hospitals.[15] At Bellevue Hospital, they were outraged to discover "patients and beds in unspeakable conditions," as described by Paul Starr in his 1982 book, _The Social Transformation of American Medicine._ There was no soap in the laundry room. Only one nurse was assigned to the surgical ward, and she slept in the bathroom. The association made the ghastly discovery that only the rodents were making hospital rounds at night.[15] This investigation became the impetus for nursing-education reform.[15]

Initially, some doctors objected to the formal training of nurses. They were threatened by the thought that educated nurses would not do as they were told. Nevertheless, many welcomed the professional training of nurses from the middle class of society.[15] Eventually, doctors not only began accepting educated nurses, they grew to rely on them and appreciate their educated contribution to the health of their patients.

A sharp increase in nursing schools resulted. In 1873, there were only three nursing schools in America. They were located in New York, New Haven, and Boston.[15] That number increased to 432 nursing schools in 1900 and nearly tripled over the next decade to 1,129 nursing schools.[15]

~*~

During the spring of 1895, Alice and her family were thrilled to see a hospital diploma nursing school developing in the neighboring town of Milwaukee. Alice was an ideal candidate. She was twenty-six years old, single, a woman of good moral character, and more importantly, of good health. After all, she would be taking care of the ill. With encouragement from her family and the people of her church, Alice applied and went for an interview. Within a month she was selected. She was pleased, and her parents, even more so.

Alice not only attended classes and tended to patients at the hospital, but she lived on the hospital grounds. Students were expected to commit at least sixty hours a week to the program. They studied anatomy, physiology, and took the ever-dreaded *materia medica* class, the course in which Alice learned about medications.[14] The content was difficult, but more difficult was the teacher, whom Alice dreaded. Were instructors plotting to eliminate nursing students from the program? It felt that way.

In addition, nursing students were expected to do most of the housekeeping chores, such as washing the linens, scrubbing the floors, and loading coal into the burners. They were responsible for mending their own uniforms.[14] They not only took care of their own hair and hygiene, they were responsible for their patients' cleanliness, too. Nurses' training was a way of life. It was truly an institutional experience.

Life is tough.

Illustration 11. Milwaukee County Hospital in the 1890s. Photo reprinted with the permission from the Milwaukee School of Engineering School of Nursing.

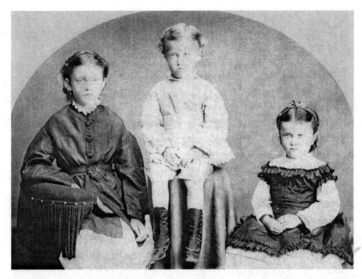

Illustration 12. Beulah, Edwin, and Alice Wood circa 1874 in Wisconsin.[5] Little Alice looks remarkably similar to the author's third daughter, Monika, at six years of age. Monika would be Alice's great-great-granddaughter.

Illustration 13. The Wood family circa 1884: From left: Alice, age sixteen; Clara French Wood, Beulah, Pierson, and Edward.

Illustration 14. Alice Ada Wood, photographed abt 1896 when she was twenty-eight, which was about the time she was attending nursing school at Milwaukee County Training School of Nursing and just before she married Gideon Ellis.[5]

Alice would be coming home for Christmas. Pierson and Clara were ecstatic. Alice's older sister, Beulah, and younger brother, Edwin, would be home too, and they were excited to hear about Alice's time at nursing school. She had been gone only a few months. The family was living in Wauwatosa, a suburb west of Milwaukee.[5]

Pierson, the stonecutter, knew the value of hard work. His expectations were high, and he was successful. He expected no less from his two daughters and son. Alice wanted to please him. Nevertheless, she felt she also needed to be honest. Nursing school was exhausting, demanding, and not what she expected. Alice was young. She thought about this as she traveled home for the Christmas holiday. She would tell her father the truth.

At Christmastime in Milwaukee, the streets were decorated with lights. Travelers excited to reunite with their families filled the train stations and city centers.

Alice and a few other students pooled their money to hire a horse and buggy to drive them home. They all lived east of Milwaukee. The ride was bitter cold. The driver provided wool blankets to protect them from the blowing wind, but their faces felt the chill. The hills glistened with snow.

Alice arrived and was welcomed home. What should she say? What would her parents do? She decided to give them a very special Christmas gift, the gift of what they wanted to hear. She shared with her family the excitement and joy of going to nursing school. It was perfect. They were pleased. Now Alice felt committed to completing her program.

Life is deceptive.

Alice returned to school in January 1896 with a new sense of obligation to her future. Nursing school was difficult, but she was determined to make it. She was steadfast. She had made a promise—not just to her family, but also to herself. She rededicated herself to the study of nursing.

She went back with a new sense of energy and commitment and eagerly settled into her hospital quarters. The aging housemother, Abigail Richards, had been a granny midwife in her younger years. She had adopted the role of housemother at the nursing school just a year earlier. She loved being with the nursing students. She was their emotional support and listening ear. When Alice left for Christmas break, Abigail knew she was struggling emotionally. When she returned, Abigail greeted her at the door and welcomed her back.

Thanks to her new sense of commitment, Alice finished her first year of nursing school near the top of her class.

Abigail was thrilled.

Illustration 15. Milwaukee County Hospital in the 1890s. Reprinted with permission from the Milwaukee School of Engineering School of Nursing.

Illustration 16. Class of 1896 at the Milwaukee County Training School of Nursing. Reprinted with the permission from the Milwaukee School of Engineering School of Nursing.

"I love you not only for what you are, but for what I am when I am with you."
~Elizabeth Barrett Browning

3

1896~Falling in Love

Gideon J. Ellis

Summertime. Alice had a very short break from nursing school. She liked to spend her off time walking on the boardwalks by the Milwaukee waterfront. The lake was polluted. Many people threw their trash into Lake Michigan. The air was dirty due to the factories. The skies were smoky. Thick, black clouds were common.[16] Stench and poverty were everywhere.

Alice knew that if she could get to the waterfront in the early hours of the day, she could minimize her exposure to the stench and crowds. She was used to a five o'clock wake-up, so it was quite natural for her to make an early trip to the waterfront from the nursing school. She appreciated the solitude of walking along Lake Michigan. She would often bring a book of poetry written by Elizabeth Browning to read. It was something very different from her demanding nursing books.

Coincidentally, others shared Alice's fondness for secluded walks—specifically, a dashing young man named Gideon J. Ellis, who was twenty-seven years old. Gideon was tall with broad shoulders. He spoke with a deep, kind, and gentle voice. He was a man's man. Gideon, who was from Michigan, came from a long line of American war heroes dating back to his great-great-grandfather, also named Gideon Ellis. The elder Gideon Ellis was born on July 21, 1759, in Harwich, Massachusetts, and had fought in the Revolutionary War.[5]

Gideon was a member of the United States Navy and would be in port until early next year. Soon he would be called to explore the world with his mates from the ship. [5]

Gideon noticed Alice immediately. Alice did not notice him. She had come to the shore to experience solitude, so she remained aloof. Gideon was patient; he would find the right way and time.

Surprisingly, Gideon found himself joining Alice on her walks within a week. At first, they did not say much. They focused instead on the natural beauty that surrounded them: the sky, the trees, the lake, and the singing birds. Nonetheless, as the weeks passed, they both knew there was a mutual attraction, and it was growing every day.

Alice was letting her guard down. What would happen if somebody found out she was dating? She knew quite well that this would be unacceptable to the nursing school as well as to her parents. She would tell no one. She could secretly date Gideon for a short time. She needed to talk, but she had no one in whom she could confide. Then she thought of Abigail, the housemother at the nursing school.

Abigail understood, though she did not approve or encourage Alice's decision to accompany Gideon on a date, for surely this could result in Alice's dismissal from the nursing program. Abigail knew Alice as a nursing student. But now it was apparent that Alice was a young woman who wanted to experience love.

Alice returned to the waterfront.

Gideon knew how to court women. He was clever. He had the advantage of traveling from seaport to seaport, where there were always young women waiting to meet a charming and handsome young man. If the relationship did not work out, he had a good excuse to exit. The sea was calling.

Shortly after they began their daily walks, they began to attend community dances. Alice found herself coming to town daily.

Abigail was not happy. She knew what Alice was doing, but chose to remain silent. School would start in a week, and surely Alice would return to her nursing studies.

This was not so.

~*~

Alice returned to school in the fall of 1896. However, she continued to meet Gideon on the waterfront after school. She did not commit herself to her studies, and after a few weeks, she was failing. Nursing school was not her priority.

Abigail knew that Alice was following her heart and not listening to her head. Almost immediately, Nurse Campbell, the superintendent of second-year nursing, called Alice in for a meeting.

Nurse Campbell spoke with Alice and demanded an answer. How did her top nursing student change so quickly? Currently, Alice was failing each of her courses.

Alice was honest. She told Nurse Campbell about Gideon and how, for the first time in her life, she felt alive. Alice was asked to leave nursing school. This was what she wanted.

This was what Gideon wanted, as well. He desired to marry

Alice. However, Gideon made it very clear that he was not interested in a marriage that included children.[5]

Alice understood.[5]

Alice's parents were furious.[5] How could she leave nursing school to be with a man whom she'd only known for a few months? Pierson demanded to speak to this immoral man.

Gideon refused.

Pierson would not leave the matter alone. He went to the docks at the shipyard and hunted Gideon down. Pierson made it clear that he held Gideon responsible for Alice's dismissal from nursing school, and therefore Gideon was responsible for her care. Pierson left in a huff. He could not speak to Alice, he was so angry.

Clara was a tough woman, and she, too, despised Gideon. On one hand, she was outraged that Alice was leaving nursing school. On the other, she was heartbroken. Clara commiserated with her sister, Callie, and her older daughter, Beulah.

It was official. Alice gathered all of her belongings and left the student nurses' quarters. Abigail gave her a big hug and told her that she could envision Alice as a pioneer nurse or midwife, and that Alice would find a place where she could offer compassionate care for others. Abigail told Alice that she would keep her in her deep thoughts and prayers.

Alice left nursing school never to return.

~*~

Alice and Gideon were married on Dec 31, 1896, in Milwaukee's city hall.[5] Alice's parents and siblings did not attend the ceremony. The couple settled in a small flat near the port of Milwaukee.

Gideon affirmed that he loved being hitched. At least in the beginning.

Alice was hesitant about their relationship. Alice could not break away from her family. She went home when she could. She was welcome at the Wood home. Gideon was not.

In the spring, it was time for Gideon to re-up for ship duty. He decided against it. Gideon knew that it was important to get Alice out of town, away from family interference.[5] Gideon had read about Deadwood, a town in the Black Hills of South Dakota. It would be an exciting move for them. George Custer, Wild Bill Hickok, and Calamity Jane each had left marks in Deadwood.[17] Goldmines were being built, and help was needed. Gideon and Alice could provide that help.

Illustration 17. Gideon Ellis and Alice Wood, at Christmas 1896, just before they married.[5]

Summer arrived. They moved and thrived. By the end of the year, they both had steady work. Gideon was an electrical engineer, and Alice offered her services as a pioneer midwife and nurse in many homes.

The citizens' of Deadwood needed medical and birthing care. Many women were there with their gold-mining husbands. Other women worked as ladies of the evening. All were away from their extended families and needed help birthing. Alice could help all of the women of Deadwood. Her experience assisting her mother, Clara, and her grandmother, Mary French, as they helped others with birthing in Milwaukee was priceless. Her midwifery, nursing skills, training and Clara's remedies armed Alice with knowledge and were valuable. They paid off—positive births were plentiful.

Until November 1897.

Alice had an unsettling birthing experience in Deadwood one night, and it remained with her always.

James and Elizabeth's Story

Alice was at home early one quiet evening in November 1897. Waiting for Gideon to return from work. A frantic knock on the door disturbed her. Alice opened the door, and there stood a frightened and trembling young miner named James. He explained that his pregnant wife was ready to give birth, but she was not doing well and needed help. Alice recognized him immediately from town.

Alice hurriedly gathered her supplies, mounted her horse, and joined James. They rode quickly through the dark, cold streets of Deadwood. At the edge of town, they took a dirt road up through the forest. A gentle breeze soughed through the trees; a full moon lit the trail as they rode.

They approached the cabin and tied up their horses. As they approached the front door, James untied a rope he had wrapped around a nail to keep the door shut.

They entered. A fire was burning in the potbellied stove. On one side of the room, there was a rocker with a basket of yarn and needles and a wooden cradle next to it. On the other side, there was a small table. The flickering flame in an oil lantern lit the room. Toward the back of the dark cabin, a pregnant woman was on her couch and moaning. This had gone on for two days. Her moans were broken and weak—not the typical sounds of a woman in labor. James had propped her up with pillows, as it seemed to ease her breathing.

As Alice approached, she immediately noticed the pregnant woman's grossly swollen arms, legs, and face. James told Alice that the swelling had just started the past week. She had been nauseated and had not eaten much. She was having pains in her abdomen. Her skin was yellow and bruised.[18, 19] This was Elizabeth.

James told Alice that his wife's vision was failing, and she had been tormented by excruciating headaches over the past month.[18, 19] A vial of opium was near.

Alice lifted the blanket and noticed the baby's head protruding. With the help of James, she removed the baby. The pale baby was lifeless; and quickly became cool to the touch. It was a boy. Alice gently wrapped the baby in a towel and handed him to the grief-stricken new father.

As Alice waited for the placenta to separate, she noticed that Elizabeth was beginning to gasp weakly. She needed more air. Simultaneously, Elizabeth began to convulse and the placenta was expelled. The gate had been opened. Blood began to drain from every orifice of Elizabeth's dying body.[18, 19] Every hair follicle was dotted with blood.

James laid his deceased baby, his son, in the wooden cradle he had made. He then walked over, sat down, and wrapped his arms around Elizabeth as her body became less responsive. Her breathing was irregular. She began to alternate between rapid breathing and the absence of breaths. Her lungs rattled with congestion.[20] Then it happened. Elizabeth stopped breathing.

James gently lifted Elizabeth's lifeless body, carried her over to the rocking chair, and wept. He could not speak.

Alice stayed with James throughout the night. She quietly cleaned the baby boy and dressed him in an outfit that Elizabeth had sewed for her new baby. She wrapped him in a fresh, homemade blanket. And then she laid him in the wooden cradle, on which James had inscribed "Rock-a-bye Baby." Alice then proceeded to gather the soiled blankets and towels and remove the blood and debris. She covered the couch with fresh towels and blankets and helped James clean Elizabeth. They laid her down on the couch.

The night had passed and dawn was breaking. The sun rose. James decided to mount his horse and retrieve the undertaker. He asked Alice to stay with Elizabeth and their deceased baby. Alice was happy to help. He stopped at Dr. Twilly's Medicine Store, where the services of undertaking and over-the-counter medical advice were offered. Dr. Twilly was the resident medical expert; his twelve-week certificate was mounted on the wall. There were no true doctors in town. Alice patiently waited for them to return.

James arrived with the undertaker, who drove a team of horses pulling a covered wagon. James walked into the cabin and lifted up Elizabeth. Then he carried her outside and gently laid her in the back of the wagon. The undertaker handed James a silk pillow to place under her head. Alice walked outside and up to the wagon and placed the baby in Elizabeth's arms. James took a family quilt and covered them both. Soon the undertaker left with both bodies. James was devastated.

Alice gave James a hug and told him to stop by. He never did.

Life is bitter.

As a new midwife, Alice spent the next few weeks trying to decipher what had happened. Were the headaches, bleeding, and yellowed skin related to Elizabeth's and her baby's untimely deaths? At times like these, she wished her mother, Clara, and Grandma French were nearby to help—or even just to listen.

~*~

By Gideon's standards, he and Alice had a decent first year for a couple of newlyweds. They argued. They fought. They made love. Conflict always seemed to be looming. Both Alice and Gideon were fiercely independent. It was a constant struggle to keep harmony in their home.

New Year's Eve arrived, and they celebrated their first anniversary on Dec 31, 1897, with a delicious meal made by Alice. Shortly thereafter, Gideon left to meet the men of the town—not exactly what Alice had in mind.

On January 1, 1898, the New Year arrived, and they both continued to work hard in their professions as well as at home, where they strived to maintain a cordial relationship.

Then it happened. Alice knew.

Alice became fretful. She could not hide. During Christmas, she had been nauseous, but the discomfort had gone away. She was with child and cautiously elated. But she dreaded telling Gideon. What would he do? She'd heard that some women tried to end their pregnancies in ways that terrified her. She feared that Gideon would insist that she do that. She decided not to tell Gideon until she had no other choice.

By February 1898, she could not keep it from him anymore. She told him the truth. She was in a family way and due in June.

Gideon was not pleased. He had taken precautions. He had purchased some lambskin products from sheep herders that he could wrap around his *best friend.* They were made from the cecum of the lamb and provided a naturalistic condom.[21] He was sure that she would not get pregnant. But she had.

The next few months were stormy.

Life is stubborn.

In May 1898, Alice was eight months pregnant. She boarded the train for Milwaukee by herself; she was packed and ready to move home. Riding the train while expectant drew attention from others—especially because she was traveling solo.

People stared.

~*~

During the Victorian Era, pregnant women were expected to withdraw from society, not to be seen or heard from. Terms such as "in a family way," "in a delicate condition," and "expectant with child" were commonly used to describe being pregnant. "Confinement" or "lying-in" described the time of labor and a ten-day to two-week period of bed rest after delivery.[23, 24]

Prolonged bed rest after birthing can lead to a propensity to develop a blood clot—a serious condition—or the less severe inflammation of the superficial veins. Both conditions typically occur in the legs. In the early 1900s, the medical community recognized that maternity-related blood clotting was linked to poor circulation, and if a clot became dislodged it posed a significant threat to the heart and lungs. What doctors didn't seem to notice then was the relationship between prolonged bed rest and the incidence of blood clots and inflammation of the superficial veins.[18, 19,]

Today, a new understanding exists. After birth, as a protective factor, a woman's ability to form clots increases.[18] This mechanism protects women from excessive blood loss after giving birth. However, the disadvantage is that women can also form unwanted blood clots in their legs. Clots sometimes form during pregnancy, but more often occur after the birth. They may or may not be related to prolonged bed rest.[18, 19, 21] This may have been a cause for maternal morbidity and mortality during the Victorian and Edwardian eras.

In 1904, medical literature stated that if an infection from the uterus traveled through the pelvis and attacked the tissues at a cellular level, phlegmasia alba dolens would result, and one or both legs would swell. Early medical scientists and the laity attributed the swelling of a woman's legs after birth to her breast milk pooling there, a condition commonly called *milk leg*.[18, 22, 23]

~*~

Alice, who was *in a family way*, arrived in Milwaukee at the train depot at dawn. She could not hide her condition. She was petrified. She needed to find her way to the Wood home, where she could talk to Pierson and Clara. She needed help.

Alice soon found a carriage with a driver. He helped her with her luggage and helped her climb into her seat. It was quite high, and being *expectant with child* made her ungainly. Alice sat down and got comfortable. She endured the bumpy ride home, praying that her bladder would survive. In the midst of all this upheaval, it was spring and lovely. Rain fell gently on the green countryside. Alice relaxed.

When Alice arrived home, Clara and Pierson were surprised. They came out to the carriage in tears to greet their daughter. They welcomed her with open arms. They took her inside and made her comfortable.

This moment of reuniting was more amicable than Alice had anticipated. She settled in. Not much was said, but Clara and Pierson could see that Alice was hurting. Had Gideon destroyed her confidence? No one but Alice—and perhaps Gideon—knew. No one spoke about the marriage.

Alice was exhausted.

A few weeks later, she was ready to birth. She had a few false pains or sporadic uterine contractions, but they were not regular.[21] She felt blessed to be home where the people who loved her most would be able to care for her during the birth of her first child. She would be with her mother, Clara, who was respected in her community for her ability to care for others during birth.

Clara disliked using the discouraging phrase "false pains." She chose to call the sporadic contractions the "uterus in training."

Alice's Birthing Story

Alice woke up one morning and she felt light contractions. Was she was having false pains? As the day continued, the contractions became more regular and intense. She told her mother, "It's time."

Clara gave Alice some towels to fold. Clara was grateful to be there for her daughter's first birth, just as her mother, Mary French, had been there for her births. She was excited to meet her new grandchild. Clara sent her son, Eddie, to notify Beulah to come home and help out with her sister's birth.

As the day progressed, so did the contractions, their power increasing. Alice started to breathe a little deeper, "wheww whewww." Alice declared, "Mama, these pains are quite strong."

Within a short time, Clara said, "Alice, come over here and stand next to the table. Now lean over with both of your hands flat on the table." Then, Clara gave Alice a bowl of bread dough to knead.

Beulah arrived and was excited to see that the confinement was progressing. She offered to help. She stood behind Alice and pushed on her back. Alice was elated to have her sister there. She welcomed her help. She welcomed her tender touch.

Then there was Pierson. He knew his role in all of this. It was time to go fishing. So he called Eddie down to accompany him to the lake. It was the first of June, and the fish were ready.

Several hours later, Alice frantically told Clara, "How can this be? Whew-whew-whew. I am ready to have a baby, and you have me kneading whew-whew-whewww—BREAD DOUGH! For the grace of God, Mama, help me—whew-whew-whew."

Clara said, "All right, child, you are getting closer. Come with me and you can lie on this bed."

Beulah knew the routine. She was in the bedroom preparing the bed with brown paper. Clara had melted wax on the paper so that the blood would roll off.

Alice sniveled, "No more, Mama, No more! WHEW-WHEW-WHEW-WHEW."

Clara looked into Alice's eyes and firmly stated, "Alice Ada Wood Ellis, look at me! Listen. Beulah will hold up two to three fingers, and you are to breathe with her, understand? Watch the fingers, Alice. Three fingers, three deep breaths. Help your baby, Alice. Help your baby breathe!"

Alice paid close attention to Beulah and her fingers. Alice called out to Clara, "WHEW-WHEW-WHEW. Mama, I can feel the baby moving down between my legs, WHEWWW. I can feel pressure!"

"This is good," Clara said. "Turn to your side." Clara made Alice wait. She knew it would be harmful to push too early.

Clara had assisted with a birth just a year prior. She had been called in on day two of an extended confinement, better known as a labor experience. The senior woman at the birth had been impatient and had the mother pushing too soon in the labor. The poor mother nearly lost her baby. Every blood vessel in her eyes was broken. After two days, the doctor was called. He said the woman was completely swollen inside and he would need to use foreceps to extract the baby. The mother and baby nearly died during that process. The baby was bruised all over. Clara knew that mothers needed to feel the push.

Clara wanted to be sure Alice was ready.

Alice was ready. "Mama I am ready! Wheww-wheww!"

Clara took action. "Pull on this towel, Alice, while I pull on the offer end, and push! Breathe, Alice. Breathe. Breathe for your baby. Breathe. Breathe while you push. Don't hold your breath. Let your bottom push your baby out, keep your mouth open."

Within several minutes, with the unyielding help of Clara and Beulah, Alice birthed her baby girl.

Alice Ada gave birth to a beautiful baby girl "Myrtle June Clarabelle Ellis" on June 1, 1898, in the Woods' home.

Clara spoke as she removed the mucous from the newborn mouth, "Alice you did it, she is beautiful, she is just perfect. Lie still and we will wait for the cord to stop pulsating, then tie it off." Very soon that happened and Clara and Beulah tied two ends of the cord off and then cut the cord. While Beulah waited for the placenta to expel, Clara brought the baby up to Alice. Baby Myrtle gazed around the room and into her momma's eyes.

What a beautiful experience for Clara to see her daughter and Beulah see her sister Alice give birth. Clara was an expert in helping a woman with child —and now with her own daughter.

During the latter part of the nineteenth century, 95 percent of American women birthed in the home. A variety of people cared for expectant mothers during births.[15, 23-24] Among them were lay midwives, such as granny midwives in the South, and trained midwives or physicians, who trained in the United States or more often received training in Europe. Unfortunately, the midwifery or physician training that practitioners received varied considerably, and there was no uniform practice.[15, 23-24]

Therefore, women were often unaware of the best practices. More importantly, historical accounts often neglected to acknowledge good birthing care provided by the woman's own family, as the Wood family had done for generations.

Clara's experience with the neighbor woman, who was told push too soon, was an example of poor practice. This case resulted in pathological swelling. When the woman pushed, it just increased the swelling even more and prohibited the baby from descending. This necessitated the use of forceps and could have resulted in a surgical delivery. This example of poor practice can happen in hospitals, too. Please note, this foul practice may still happen in some twenty-first century homes and hospitals.[5] Eventually, cases like this one drew the attention of legislators and the medical community. In the late 1890s, however, midwifery laws often followed local custom rather than the state or national standards.[22-24] This was even truer in the West, where legislation related to maternity practice was in its infancy.

A birthing caregiver's, and her closest contemporaries, lived experiences of birthing were her case studies. It was of the utmost importance that the person providing birthing care could discern good practice. The Wood family used good practices.[5] More importantly, they used discernment.[5] They were known and respected in the community for their ability to assist in this endeavor.

Illustration 18. Clara Wood with her granddaughter, Myrtle, who was about three months old, in Milwaukee, Wisconsin, September 1898.[5]

In November 1898, five months after baby Myrtle was born, Gideon showed up unexpectedly at the Wood home. He was repentant. He wanted to meet his daughter. It was getting cold, and he wanted his wife to be with him. He hired a horse and buggy to drive him from the Milwaukee train depot to the Wood home. He told the driver not to leave. He had just bought a new baby dress for Myrtle.

When he arrived at the Wood home, Alice led him into the front parlor. He lifted Myrtle and began to play with her.

Myrtle reciprocated and smiled.

He expressed remorse to Alice and pleaded for her forgiveness. He wanted his wife and his baby to return to Deadwood, South Dakota, with him, and he would do whatever was necessary convince Alice to go. He promised that he had changed.

Gideon and Clara spoke only a few words. Pierson refused to talk to Gideon or Alice. Within two hours, Alice and her five-month-old baby were loaded on the buggy with Gideon to return to South Dakota. Clara was despondent.

Pierson and Clara did not hear from Alice the next year. Neither did her sister Beulah. They each wanted to talk to Alice and see if she was well. Even more, they wanted to see and hold their grandbaby and niece. They were gravely concerned and suffered many sleepless nights.

Gideon and Myrtle June Ellis

Illustration 19. Gideon Ellis with his oldest daughter, Myrtle June Ellis, in 1899, just prior to the breakup of his marriage.[5]

A year later, in December 1899, Alice returned once more to the Wood home with Myrtle, who was now eighteen months old.

Pierson and Clara were wary but nevertheless elated to see Alice and their beautiful granddaughter, Myrtle, who was now walking. It appeared to Pierson and Clara that Alice's heart had been trampled, and they grieved for that.

Not much was said.

Except one thing.

Alice firmly declared, "I will never spend one more minute of my life with Gideon. I am finished. This is not a marriage worth saving. I am done."

Soon, "Happy New Year" was heard around the world. It was January 1, 1900. A new century commenced. Excitement filled the streets. Everyone was making impressive plans for the new century. Everyone except Alice, that is.

It had happened.

Alice knew, just as she had known two years earlier. She felt nauseated at Christmas, and by January she had started to heave. It was the same as last time. In the morning she would get queasy, and then soon she would retch. She knew she was expectant with child again. How did this happen? Being a single woman with a toddler was a challenge, but being a single mother with a toddler and a baby? Unthinkable.

Life is a struggle.

It would be difficult to tell her father. Her mother would understand, but Pierson would not.

March 1900 came along. Alice was nervous that Gideon might return and ashamed that she was expectant with child again. She had left nursing school abruptly to get married. Was she a disgrace to her family? What did worshippers at church think? What should she do?

She needed a fresh start. She needed to move on and find a place where she could succeed and live as a single mother with two children.

Alice, who was seven months pregnant, read the newspapers that Pierson brought home. She began to read about the Seattle Klondike Gold Rush. It seemed promising. The headlines were captivating. There was still gold in the Alaska-Yukon region, and Seattle needed help outfitting the miners. Alice felt this might work for her and the girls, as well as her parents.

She just needed to talk to her father. What would Pierson think? Pierson was not exactly happy with her choices of late.

To Alice's surprise, not only was Pierson interested, but also he had been investigating the same thing. In fact, he was going to a town hall meeting that night at the rail depot to hear a man talk about opportunities available to people interested in moving west. Flyers advertised meetings everywhere. The railroads were interested in convincing people to move to the West and "invest in their future."

Pierson was sold. He came back from the meeting brimming with anticipation. He had always been an explorer at heart. The very next day, he put the family home up for sale. The whole family would be moving.

Life is exhilarating.

During the month of May, the Wood home sold. The buyers planned to return in December and move in. The Woods could live there until then and pay rent.

Alice's Second Birthing Story

On June 6, 1900, Alice gave birth to very healthy baby girl. She named her Beulah Marie Ellis after Alice's sister, Auntie Beulah. This time during labor, Clara and Beulah did not have Alice knead bread dough, but they did have her churn butter. Many of the tasks that Clara used with Alice during childbirth, such as folding clothes and kneading dough, were not only practical but were what we might now call "evidence-based practice." They distracted the mother from the pain and allowed women to move in a rocking motion and remain upright—all while caring out a meaningful task. A good expenditure of energy.

Alice could not believe Clara and Beulah's unorthodox birthing methods. She was astounded. Alice vowed that she would never have the women she helped with birthing do these tasks during labor.

Life is comical.

Alice would call the new baby Marie. A few weeks later, when Marie was baptized at the local Methodist church, the congregation was kind and supportive. A few days after the baptism, Pierson, Eddie and Beulah left for Seattle to find work and a temporary place for the family to live.

Alice finalized her divorce from Gideon in August 1900. Gideon had rejoined the navy and would ship out after Christmas.[5]

In November, Gideon stopped by the Wood home to finalize their relationship.[5] He did love his little girl, Myrtle. She was so darned adorable. He suggested to Alice that he could take Myrtle and she could keep the baby.[25, 5]

Alice thought, *Think again, Gideon! Over my dead body! No way will you take either girl—now or ever!*

Alice carefully explained to Gideon that his suggestion was nonsensical and that only she could care for the girls. He would be out at sea and thus, he would not be able to be a father. This was true.

Gideon decided to cut and run.

As he left the Wood home, Alice said, "Gideon, don't you want to see the new baby, Marie?"[5]

He grunted, walked over to the cradle, flipped the blanket away, and said nothing. He opened the door and left.[5] He was not pleased.

Alice was relieved. She knew they needed to scoot out of town in a scuttle.[25] She could not trust Gideon. He might be back. Clara, the girls, and she would be leaving on a locomotive steam train bound for Saint Paul and then on to Seattle, where Pierson would be waiting.

December came and they left Wisconsin, never to return.

Life is daunting.

Alice did indeed fall in love—with her two beautiful daughters, Myrtle and Marie, whom she could count on as she proceeded to live her life as she chose. In addition, she gained a new admiration and love for her own parents, Pierson and Clara.

Alice was maturing.

Illustration 20. Mount Rainier looms over Seattle in this photograph taken in 1900 by Anders Willse. Denny Hill stands approximately where the Seattle Space Needle is today. Denny Hill was leveled to provide landfill for Seattle's Harbor Island, which is the port where cargo ships dock. Reprinted per permission from the MOHAI.

"A pioneer is not someone who makes her own soap. She is one who takes up her burdens and walks toward the future."
~Laurel Thatcher Ulrich in A Midwife's Tale

4

1900~Arriving in Seattle & Green Lake

Magnificent

The spirit of Christmas had arrived in Seattle. The train depot was filled with folks waiting to greet their loved ones. On December 25, 1900, Pierson and Eddie welcomed Clara, Alice, and the girls to Seattle. Pierson had arranged for them to stay at a boarding house near the train station. Clara's humpback trunk, which Pierson had made, was the first one unloaded from the train cargo container.

So clever.

~*~

Seattle's population was rapidly growing. It could be defined as a boomtown. In 1900, more than 80,000 people lived there.[6, 7] Seattle was the gateway to Alaska and the Yukon. While the miners were mining the mines, Seattleites were mining the miners.[6, 7, 26]

Seattle in the early 1900s most people walked, rode in carriages, took streetcars or even pedaled modern, chain-driven bicycles to get around. In 1900 there was only one car in the Seattle, a Wood's Electric, built by Ralph Hopkin, who drove the car to Seattle from Chicago. Shortly thereafter, automobiles began appearing on Seattle's unpaved city streets. However, the autos, or horseless carriages, were frequently rickety and had thin tires. They often got stuck in the mud. It was common to hear the call, "Get a horse!" [26]

Most people relied on runners or couriers to send "instant" messages locally and used the post office for less urgent ones. Telephones were a novelty, and rudimentary telephone services were poorly connected. Telegraphs sent via companies like Western Union connected Seattleites to the outside world.[26] Newspapers depicted the everyday and personal lives of Seattle citizens, at times revealing shocking and provocative news.

~*~

The morning after they arrived in Seattle, Clara stayed in the boarding house with the girls so that Pierson and Alice could explore. Eddie stopped by and shared that he would be heading north to Bellingham to investigate a new job. Beulah was sleeping in one of the rooms and did not visit much, not feeling well. Clara felt Beulah was despondent and worried about her future. Regardless, it was great to know that the whole family made the journey out to the West.

Pierson told Alice, "Let's go trekking. We have lots of ground to cover. Make sure you put on your boots. It might be muddy."

So under her long skirt, Alice buttoned up her boots. She was a lady at first glance, but at heart she was a daring explorer ready to take on adventure. She grabbed her jacket. She was ready to join her father and explore Seattle.

They started off with a hike up Denny Hill. The fog was lifting. Alice was strong and an excellent hiker, easily keeping pace with her strong father. They reached the top of the hill. The morning was crisp, and to the south, the sky was blue. They could see for miles. Mount Rainier appeared to be floating above the cityscape. They could barely believe their eyes. They stood before this majestic volcanic mountain in awe.

Pierson wanted to show his daughter a place he hoped they could all call home. They took a series of streetcars and a trolley north to an up-and-coming Seattle neighborhood called Green Lake.

Illustration 21. Downtown Seattle in the early 1900s. The first car arrived in Seattle in 1900. Permission granted from the University of Washington, Special Collections, Warner 3021.

It was wet and cold. The day after Christmas is not the best time of year to enjoy the weather in Seattle. However, by Wisconsin standards, it was mild. Seattle would do just fine. Father and daughter were particularly drawn to the east side of the lake.

Illustration 22. Green Lake Trolley in 1891. Permission granted from the University of Washington, Special Collections, LaRoche61.

Pierson told Alice that a man with the same surname as theirs, William D. Wood, was developing Green Lake into a desirable place to live.[28]

~*~

William D. Wood had been the mayor of Seattle since 1896. During July 1897, he was attending a convention in San Francisco when the steamship *Excelsior* arrived in San Francisco Bay carrying in heaps of gold.[6, 7] Two days later, on

July 17, 1897, Wood received word that the *SS Portland* had arrived in Seattle loaded with two tons of gold and precious metals.[6, 7] Immediately, he telegraphed city hall in Seattle, resigning his position as mayor and joined the gold rush stampede.[7, 28] Bypassing Seattle, he quickly headed north to Alaska.

This would be the start of one of many profitable ventures for Wood—transporting miners and supplies via ferries from San Francisco to Seattle and then on to the Yukon mining fields. He had moved to Seattle from the San Francisco Bay area, and it is possible that he'd maintained close ties with business associates in California. Wood played a crucial role in the formation of the Seattle Yukon Trading Company, and he continued to work as a land speculator and attorney.[7, 28]

Illustration 23. William D. Wood (1858 – 1917) in 1898. Courtesy of the Seattle Municipal Archives.

~*~

Pierson and Alice walked the streets of East Green Lake. It was muddy. A few homes were half built, but construction had been halted for the Christmas season. Pierson told Alice he had a surprise.

Alice was leery. She thought—What by the grace of God did my father do? "So, Father, tell me the surprise. I'm ready."

"Not yet," Pierson responded. "Soon."

This was frustrating for Alice. Why did her father even mention a surprise? She reverted to the daughter she had been when she was young. She begged and pleaded, and her softhearted father gave in.

"Alice, I have great news for you and your mother. Just walk up this street, and I will show you."

They walked up the street, and Pierson showed Alice the two lots he had purchased. He planned for them to build their homes right next to each other.[5]

Alice had to think. She was grateful for father's gift, but she wanted to have a greater role in deciding where they would live.

Illustration 24. East Green Lake in 1904. Notice the grammar school on the left. Permission granted from the University of Washington, Special Collections, UW14542.

Illustration 25. Green Lake Trolley in 1897. (Courtesy of Seattle Municipal Archives, 29246.)

Pierson told Alice, "I can imagine you wanted to take part in this purchase. But in just six months, the price of these lots has grown significantly. I had to make a move fast."

Alice understood.

"The good news, Alice, is that you can decide on a builder and design your home all by yourself. I thought I would leave it up to Clara to design our home, particularly the colors. Women need to pick the colors!" said Pierson.[5] Pierson then shared with Alice that he had arranged for the family to stay in the boarding house in Seattle until their homes were built. They returned to Seattle and settled into the boarding house and shared the news of Green Lake with Clara.

———

Sadly, an unforeseen tragedy occurred. Just two months after Clara, Alice and the girls had arrived in December 1900. On February 15, 1901, Beulah died in her sleep from unknown causes. She was buried at Lakeview Cemetery in Seattle.[5] Clara was saddened to see her pass so young, just thirty-seven years of age. They all mourned for Beulah, Clara was saddened that she had never married.[5]

———

As spring 1901 arrived Pierson and Clara started to build their home. At the beginning of the summer in 1901, they all moved to Green Lake.[5] It was exciting to be in the grassroots of a budding community. The whole family moved into Pierson and Clara's home. Alice's would start building her home next.

Alice began to help women of the community with birthing in their homes and share her mother Clara's practical medical remedies. She was starting to earn a fine reputation and income among the locals.

The whole family loved Green Lake. It was close enough to town for access to shops and other necessities, yet far enough away from the noise and chaos of the bustling city. The wild blackberries were abundant and used in many meals. Residents of Green Lake were dedicated to ensuring that the development included quality schools, parks, and a sense of community.

William Wood had donated land for the original Green Lake school in the 1890s.[28, 29] By 1902, however, the enrollment of 445 students was eleven times greater than the thirty-eight students who were enrolled in 1891. By the time the new school opened in 1902, enrollment had increased to 570 students. In 1907, enrollment had increased again to 912. The school was a solid structure. James Stephens was the developer.[29]

Illustration 26. Green Lake Grammar School in 1902. Permission granted from the University of Washington, Special Collections, photograph by Asahel Curtis. Neg.# A. Curtis 04315.

Myrtle started at Green Lake Grammar School in 1903, and Marie, in 1905. It was just a few blocks from where they lived.[5] The whole family was excited and very involved with the school as it developed.[5]

In 1900, when Pierson arrived in Seattle, he found work doing odd jobs, helping where needed with his stonecutting skills.[5, 30, 31] The city of wooden buildings had been destroyed in the Great Fire of June 6, 1889.[6] Citizens were rebuilding the city with stone and brick.[30] This was beneficial for Pierson. His stonecutting expertise was valuable, and he gained the admiration of the men working for the city of Seattle. He often did contract jobs for the city. By 1905, Pierson had found employment with the city of Seattle, and at the ripe age of sixty-nine he started a new career as a laborer.[5, 31]

Illustration 27. Seattle's Great Fire of 1889. (Library of Congress.)

Several years later, in 1904, Alice and the girls moved into their own home. Even though, their home would not be completed until 1907.[5] Alice knew that she would need to work to provide for her daughters, but she was uncertain as to how to use her skills to earn a living. Pierson had a friend in the Seattle street department whose wife was a nurse at the hospital in Seattle. She arranged for Alice to meet the director of nursing.

The very next week, Alice met with the director, who, like many directors of nursing at the turn of the twentieth century, was a nun.[5]

Clara had sewn a professional-looking dress for Alice to wear. Alice slipped on only one petticoat with this dress. It was floor length and the neckline was high. It was modest, yet pleasing to the eye—perfect for a first encounter with a nun.

Alice took the trolley down to Seattle and the streetcar to the downtown Seattle Hospital. The office was on the main floor.

Alice spoke with the director of nursing, Sister Mary Agnes. Sister Mary wanted to help Alice, but Alice had not graduated and they had plenty of help now that they had started a nursing school.

Alice understood, but she was reasonably disappointed. She knew that Sister Mary was bound by the rules of the hospital and the state. She thanked the director for her time and then walked down the hall.

A moment later, Sister Mary called to her, "Wait, Alice. I have an idea that may help you. We have a doctor here that lives by you in Green Lake. His name is Dr. Harry Brown. He is a general practitioner who has a special interest in maternity care. Would you like to talk to him?"

Alice was thrilled at the prospect. "Of course!" she
exclaimed. Sister Mary arranged for Alice to meet Dr. Brown
that very day within two hours.

Illustration 28. 1900 Providence Hospital in Seattle, Washington.
Permission granted from the University of Washington, Special
Collections, UW340.

Dr. Harrison Emmett Brown was excited to meet Alice and learn that she was his neighbor in Green Lake. She explained that she had one year of nurse's training at Milwaukee County Hospital.[5] He was pleased with this information. She also explained that she was a recent widow with two small girls. He replied, "Alice, I am glad that you have training in nursing, but what about childbirth? Do you have any experience in helping women give birth?"

Alice replied, "Oh yes, I trained with the best! My mother and grandmother. They were highly respected women in Wisconsin. Additionally, I did do some midwifing in the Black Hills gold-mining communities. I learned a lot there. However, I must say that now that I have my little girls to worry about, I do like to stay close to home."

Dr. Brown was silent for some time. Then his eyes got bigger and he exclaimed, "Alice, I have a plan! As you know, nearly all birthing happens in the comfort of a woman's own home. However, there are a few women in Seattle who are in a situation where that is not possible. Ever since the Klondike Gold Rush, we have seen a rise in women of the evening. You know—prostitutes.[5, 27] Sadly, prostitutes do get pregnant. Sisters of Providence offer care to many of these woman who are impoverished. However, a great number of these prostitutes are not impoverished. In fact, many are affluent.[27] They do not want charity, nor are they charity cases. They often struggle to find a place to give birth. Perhaps they could birth in your home. Would this interest you?"

Alice replied, "I am not sure. I have never considered this. My concern is my family and neighbors, of course."

Dr. Brown responded, "I completely understand. I am a general practitioner here at Providence Hospital. However, I am committed to helping those who are underserved, especially if it relates to maternity care. Your home is in close proximity to mine, and I could conveniently act as a consultant and tend to some of the births. Let me go down the hall and give you some time to think about this.

Alice pondered. She had given birthing care to prostitutes in Deadwood, South Dakota. They were not bad customers and they paid well. Then, she thought about her children and her parents. This would give her an opportunity to work out of her home and be close to her daughters as well as to her parents, if she needed assistance.

Additionally, Alice had compassion for others regardless of their situation. She could help. She would help these women in her own home and provide them with meals. Alice loved to cook. When Dr. Brown returned, Alice stated, "Dr. Brown, I can do this. I want to help those women and I know how. We can make this work." They spent several months making plans.

Illustration 29. Alice, Myrtle and Marie are on the porch of Alice's Green Lake home, on the left. Pierson and Clara's home is on the right.[5]

"Character cannot be developed in ease and quiet. Only through experience of trial and suffering can the soul be strengthened, ambition inspired, and success achieved."
~Helen Keller

5

1904~Making a Living

Midwifing & Nursing in the Home

It wasn't going to be easy. Alice hoped it would be worth it. She had decided to put her nursing and midwifery skills into practice. Seattle had grown rapidly over the past decade, and people needed health care. Hospitals were expanding, but a shortage existed. Dr. Brown was supportive of making Alice's home a place to give birth.[5] Alice was a widow, correct? And as a young, single mother of two daughters—Myrtle was now six years old and Marie, now four—her employment options were limited. This plan to help women give birth in her home would work. Pierson and Clara lived next door, which was convenient, as the girls could be sent next door during the births.

Alice had spoken with many people involved in health care, and she quickly created a working plan for her home. Doc Brown was most helpful and gave suggestions regarding her plan.

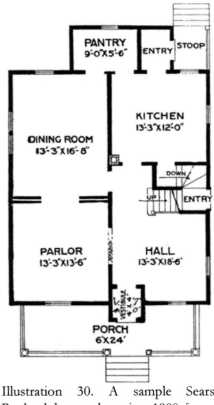

The house had four rooms and a pantry on the main floor. It was a simple design. As one entered, there was a large hall, and to the left was a parlor. The back of the house had a large dining room and kitchen. Alice made the hall

Illustration 30. A sample Sears Roebuck house plans circa 1900. [5]

into a small sitting room and placed two beds in the parlor.

In the dining room, she made a treatment/birthing room, where she kept all of her birthing supplies. Alice loved to cook and was excited to use her nice kitchen and pantry to provide her customers with home-cooked meals. As for the girls, when life got busy, they could eat next door with their grandparents. There was a small table in the kitchen, where the women would be invited to eat. From her mother, Alice had learned to get mothers walking short distances after birth, a practice that many people frowned upon at that time.[22] There were three bedrooms upstairs for Alice and her girls.

Alice was skilled. In school, she had excelled in all of her courses and hospital experiences. She had only completed one year of training, but in 1900, that was sufficient to claim she was pioneer-practical nurse. [5] The people of Seattle needed help.

In Milwaukee County, where Alice had trained as a nurse, they used the Bellevue model.[14] In the Bellevue model, the term "midwife" was used to describe a birth attendant. Additionally, Milwaukee had started a midwifery school primarily for immigrant women.[20] However, in Seattle, several people warned Alice not to use the word "midwife." Dr. Brown told Alice that some people perceived midwives as untrained and often unclean. Certain midwives were said to practice witchcraft.[23, 24] The word midwife could lower her status and hamper her ability to earn money.

Alice was compelled to agree. She needed to support her family. She did not have the luxury of time or money to fight the system. So she advertised in the paper as a nurse for hire, in her home. [5]

~*~

In 1900, only 5 percent of births took place in a hospital.[24] Ninety-five percent of birthing was in the home, and physicians attended around 50 percent of those births. Alice provided two options. A doctor with a black bag could come to Alice's home to attend the birth. Or women could give birth under Alice's care. Regardless of which option a mother selected, Alice would offer lying in for the mother and baby for seven to ten days following the birth.[5] She provided three home-cooked meals a day, clean bedding, and towels. Alice had a few chickens in her back yard and always had fresh eggs to offer.[25, 5]

Alice did not assist women to give birth in their own homes, unless it was a very close neighbor. She needed to be close to her daughters and parents. Most women preferred to birth in their own homes, so the women Alice most often took into her own house were prostitutes.[5]

These women were known as good-time girls, ladies of the evening, or harlots.[27] They were good customers and paid well. Prostitution was a growing business in Seattle, as well as in Alaska and the Yukon.[27] Inevitably, many became pregnant. Where do prostitutes give birth? For some, the Sisters of Charity of Providence Hospital in Seattle was the answer.[33] In 1878, Mother Joseph designed and supervised the building and operation of Seattle's first hospital, which was located at the corner of Fifth and Madison Streets. The order's primary mission was to serve the sick and indigent, but as the only hospital in Seattle, it also served the affluent.[33]

Prostitutes did not see themselves as charity cases. Many were affluent—some prostitutes were the highest-paid women in the West.[26] But they were not socially accepted. These prospering women were looking for a place to end their confinement and give birth, particularly when birthing in their own homes—brothels—was not desirable.

Illustration 31. Front Street in Dawson in the Yukon in 1900. Permission granted from the University of Washington, Special Collections, Photographer Eric Hegg 2333.

~*~

The Klondike Gold Rush Stampede offered the prospect of making a large sum of money quickly. There were two ways to make cash. First was mining—second was mining the miners.[26] Most of the prostitutes drawn to Alaska-Yukon were young and healthy. Like the men drawn there, they were often seeking adventure and fortune.[27]

A few of the prostitutes claimed to have met Jack London when he passed through Dawson City. He was unknown as an author at that point, yet his prowess as an explorer was recognized. He was a strikingly handsome young man from San Francisco. At the time, he was ill and not up to a social life.[34-37]

After the announcement of gold in the Yukon, Jack London, twenty-one, was one of the first explorers to travel the inside passage to Skagway, ascend the Chilkoot Pass, trek down the Klondike River, and make his way to Dawson. He spent the winter living on preserved foods in a cabin. He did not find gold. When the ice melted and spring came, he found himself broke and sick with scurvy. He returned via the Yukon River and when he hit the Bering Sea, he convinced a steamship captain to hire him to stuff coal as he traveled back to San Francisco.[34-37] He failed to return with gold, but instead he brought vivid accounts of the Yukon that he would share with many generations of readers.

In the 1900s many young women were excited to read about Jack's Yukon experience in his book, *Call of the Wild*, published in 1903. Many women during this time, loved to read about his scandalous love life and his adventures wandering the globe, which were published in the newspaper. He recently had divorced and had married an adventurous woman.[34-37]

That year, on May 5, 1906, Jack London was sent out as a special correspondent for *Collier's*, a national weekly, to write a detailed account of the aftermath of one of the twentieth century's most horrendous disasters—the great San Francisco Earthquake.[37]

Jack London and his wife, Charmain, saddled up forty miles away from San Francisco in their home of Glen Ellen. They rode into town to catch a train to Santa Rosa, then on into the city. Arriving in San Francisco, they set out on foot to investigate the atrocious disaster of the earthquake and subsequent fire. [34-37]

"Within an hour after the earthquake shock, the smoke of San Francisco's burning was a lurid tower visible a hundred miles away. And for three days and nights this lurid tower swayed in the sky, reddening the sun, darkening the day, and filling the land with smoke..." Jack London wrote in "The Story of an Eyewitness."[34]

This massive earthquake and fire resulted in more than 3,000 deaths and left 200,000 people—more than half of the city's population—homeless.[34-37]

Many Seattleites despaired, as many had relatives living in

San Francisco. Even Doc Brown and his family were affected. His childhood home on Nob Hill had been destroyed, and two of his cousins had perished.

Illustration 32. Jack London, (Library of Congress.)

~*~

In Victorian America, most women were living under societal constraints, buttoning up their shoes under two ankle-length petticoats and restructuring their abdominal organs by strapping on whalebone corset to attain the coveted small waistline.[27] However, during the Civil War, many women were forced to step out of their protective homes and seek work. The restrictions of the Victorian Era were being challenged, and the

Klondike Gold Rush gave women an opportunity to break free.[27]

A gender disparity existed in Alaska and the Yukon. In many communities, the population was more than 80 percent male.[26] Rather than looking at the social decay and menace that prostitution would bring, community leaders in the Far North took a practical approach. By legitimizing the institution of prostitution, they could satisfy the lust and desires of the male-dominated public, and they could protect their highly regarded respectable women from the violence and aggression of a woman-hungry populace.[27]

Physical stamina was required to ascend the Chilkoot Pass to the Yukon. Perhaps because of this, the health of the prostitutes was better than one might find in America's inner cities during the early twentieth century. Therefore, it was thought that there would be fewer cases of French pox, or venereal diseases, in these isolated communities.[27] At times this was true. Additionally, many of the prostitutes had to pass a health inspection before traveling to the Far North.[27]

Prostitution is one of the few professions where the best workers are often the amateurs. Although the high-risk lifestyle led to an increase in murder and suicide, many prostitutes flourished financially.[27] Some said prostitution was not much different than being in an abusive marriage, except that they were more independent and had their own income.

Some adventurous pioneer women went to Alaska and the Yukon to perform in shows, saloons, or dance halls, and do laundry or sell supplies as their day jobs. Some of these women also supplemented their incomes with prostitution.

Typically, pregnant prostitutes were forced to change their living arrangements. In brothels, it was bad for business for women to try to work during the end of their or even seen walking around the streets of the small towns.

This was too "motherly" for most men.

Instead, many of these women chose to travel to Seattle to live out the end of their pregnancies. They lived in brothels on the Seattle waterfront.[5] The brothels often provided sleeping for four or five women in one room.[27] Affluent prostitutes could afford their own rooms. Seattle offered a place where they could live virtually unnoticed during pregnancy. Wearing draping apparel, they could continue to work in darkened rooms and slip out the back door, disappearing in the crowded streets. Nevertheless, crying babies or women in labor were bad for business. Some prostitutes chose to give birth in the hospital, either as a charity case or as a paying patient, which was quite expensive. Alice gave the ladies of the evening an alternative choice, and it was not always about the money.

Alice knew how to birth. Alice was aware of the new trend toward greater medicalization of the birth process in the hospital, which was considered higher-quality care. Nevertheless, she knew that the women in her home were also receiving high-quality care based on positive maternal and infant outcomes. More importantly, her women knew this to be true.

Alice requested that each expectant woman bring a birthing companion—usually another prostitute who lived at the brothel. Ever since the tragedy that she'd experienced in Deadwood, she valued the extra set of hands. However, there were times when a woman was dropped off to fend for herself.[5] This caused anguish for Alice, as well as for the women ready to give birth.

At times, the women told Alice what they had experienced or heard was happening at hospital birthing. One of the complaints was that birthing often was managed by men or by women who were not familiar with birth. These hospital providers sometimes interpreted behaviors during labor, such as panting, moaning, or using profanity, as immodest or vulgar.[5] At times, hospital staff told women they were vulgar and to be quiet.[5] This thinking did not sit well with prostitutes or even with any women.

During birthing, Alice often thought of the mantra that had been used for many years by mothers, including Clara, which was "move the mom, move the baby."[5] Alice had learned from Clara that women needed to move and work with their baby in harmony as the baby descended through the birth canal.

Alice recognized that it was important for women to breathe

with their contractions, to work with them.[5] She knew that most women were vocal during labor.[5]

Life is considerate.

It was not long before Alice's reputation and business grew. She was well respected as a pioneer midwife/nurse who had expertise. Since she had hospital training, the medical community respected her, too.[5] Her one-year of nursing school was paying off. She knew the importance of cleanliness, and her knowledge of medical jargon made her credible among the medical profession.[5] She worked with doctors, and mutual respect grew.

Initially, Doc Brown and Alice were suspicious of one another, but soon their professional relationship developed into one of mutual trust. They each possessed numerous birthing experiences and a superior education. Alice's one year of science classes at the Milwaukee County School of Nursing surpassed the science education acquired by most nurses or even physicians practicing in America during the early 1900s.[15, 23, 24]

Dr. Harry E. Brown was born into a wealthy family in Nob Hill, a prominent neighborhood in San Francisco. His family had gained its fortune during the 1849 California Gold Rush. They owned a small manufacturing company. Their primary products were mining pans and other tools used by the prospectors panning for gold. They transported their wares to forty-niner gold-rush towns, such as Rough and Ready and Placerville, California. Other successful merchants, such as Levi Strauss, who sold canvas tarps and wagon coverings, and John Studebaker, who sold wheelbarrows to miners, also set up shop in Placerville. Philip Armour built sluices to control the water flow around the towns that supported the mines.[32] Great industrial companies rose from these clever entrepreneurs who supplied the mining booms. Mining the miners, once again.

The affluent Brown family sent their oldest son, Harry, to New York to receive a proper medical education. He trained at Bellevue Hospital in New York City, which was comparable to the hospital in which Alice trained in Milwaukee.[15, 24] The skills and the medical jargon he had learned were incredibly similar to Alice's. Doc Brown lived in Green Lake with his family and did not mind stopping by Alice's when needed.

The community of Green Lake and Alice's neighbors and friends from church had mixed feelings about her running a maternity home in their neighborhood. Most knew she was a widow and needed to earn a living, and they were supportive of her home-based endeavor. Others, especially some of her close neighbors, did not like the women who were drawn to Alice's home and their streets.

Alice did not spend much time worrying about this. She needed to provide for herself and her young family. There was a need in Seattle for her skills, and she was there to answer the call.

A few of the Klondike women had chosen to work as prostitutes just long enough to make some gold rush cash, buy a house, or pay for an education.[27] Prostitution was a lucrative business.[27] They were appreciative of Alice's services and compensated her well.

Nevertheless, like hospital birth attendants, Alice faced the additional challenge of caring for women who harbored disease and experienced illnesses or trauma too great for the body to defend or mend on its own. This would often necessitate the services of a trained provider. Fortunately, most women, most of the time, were able to utilize their own innate properties, which could offer them protection and even repair.

Alice recognized the delicate changes that occurred during the natural state of pregnancy, birthing, and feeding. She knew that the newborn separated into its own being. She understood these concepts not only as a woman who assisted others with birthing, but through her own experience of giving birth. This awareness allowed her to devise and encourage birthing practices, such as deep breathing and movement, which allowed healthy births to transpire.

Pregnancy, Birthing, and Feeding

Birth is a time when a woman, in essence, is embodied in this temporal experience that is impressively *natural* to the human flesh.[38]

Pregnancy: Throughout parturition or pregnancy, a woman takes on the spatiality of a new "being" developing inside her body. The fetus develops in a space shared with the woman. As the fetus's body grows and develops inside of its mother, the woman and fetus move in a harmonized fashion. The fetus and woman accommodate one another in their growing communal space. Uterine growth is dependent on the organ's elastic properties, which are generated by hormonal growth factors initiated after implantation of the embryo.[38] Uterine contractions, which even occur in a non-pregnant state, increase in frequency and intensity throughout the pregnancy. Often a woman is unaware of these early quiescent events until they are amplified in the later part of her pregnancy. The woman's cardiovascular system increases threefold in size. The woman's intake of nutrition, chemicals (i.e. medications), and earthly gases (i.e. oxygen) can result in beneficial or devastating outcomes for both mother and child.[18] The fetus is a foreign tissue from the same species that has a different genetic makeup that the mother has. Remarkably, the woman's body usually does not reject the fetus. Typically, the fetus remains in utero per immunological privilege, and no rejection ensues. Toward the end of the pregnancy, the woman's body often is compromised as the expanding fetus compresses the bladder and lungs.[18, 38]

Birthing: Birth takes on a new sense of embodiment as the woman and fetus end their synchronized relationship and complete the immense undertaking of becoming two separate beings through expulsion. The woman and fetus work together in a harmonizing fashion to accomplish this feat. The uterus becomes an activated spherical structure, which expands and contracts as needed for the birth to commence.[18] If the woman can relax, a normal physiological birth can progress without concern. As the fetus leaves the uterine cavity, the one becomes two—though not entirely.[38]

Feeding: As the woman engages in the shared undertaking of breast-feeding, the embodiment continues as the mother experiences the infant like an appendage.[18] During pregnancy, a cascade of hormonal changes—and not suckling or milk removal—produces milk.[18] After expulsion, the breast develops a liquid substance that has a high concentration of immunoglobulin A. This provides protection from infection for the newborn.[18] The newborn regulates the supply of milk by suckling as the breasts are emptied. Initially, successful breast-feeding is not a passive activity. The mother must engage mentally with the infant.[43] As the woman thinks about the infant or hears the infant cry, hormones are released and reflexes may be stimulated to release milk to the newborn. On the other hand, if the woman experiences stress, fear, or excessive alcohol consumption, the feeding process is hampered. During lactation, the baby anchors itself on the breast and the woman's body provides fluids, nutrients, and protective agents uniquely created for her baby.[18, 38]

Newborn's State: In a natural state, we know that the newborn is immunologically naïve and that it is dependent on its mother's defense system. In utero, a white, cheesy substance protects the fetus from maceration by the amniotic fluid. It provides warmth and insulation. It helps the fetus retain water and electrolytes. At delivery, the substance facilitates the passage of the baby through the birth canal by decreasing friction.[18] With the full-term newborn, the heaviest layers are found on the face, ears, shoulders, sacral region, and inguinal folds. If left on the infant, the substance eventually hardens and falls off. It is considered a natural moisturizer. It is also thought to have properties that promote fetal wound healing.[18, 38]

Mothers and infants have natural properties and protective mechanisms that shield them from hazards[18] These innate properties and mechanisms have always existed, making birthing possible in the most dire conditions.

ALL READY TO LEAVE SKAGWAY FOR A FAST
RUN THROUGH TO DAWSON · 600 MILES AWA

Illustration 33. Skagway in 1898, photographed by Eric Hegg
Permission granted from the University of Washington, Special
Collection, Hegg541.

"Every child is conceived either in love or lust, is born in pain, followed by joy or sometimes remorse."
~Jennifer Worth in *Call the Midwife*

6

1906~Gaining a Son

Harlots from the Yukon & Alaska

Summer was a beautiful time of the year in the Pacific Northwest. The days were mild and warm—gentle breezes cooled the region at night. The winds would blow across Green Lake making evening walks around the lake a treasured summer activity for residents. Green Lake was developing nicely. Seattle was committed to investing in quality public schools. Myrtle, eight, and Marie, six, had had a wonderful year at Green Lake School.[5] Now it was June, and summer was beginning. It was time to have fun and go to the lake. Most days, however, Alice was busy, and Clara was tired. The girls had to play close to the house until Alice or Clara could take them to the lake.[5]

Alice was very busy caring for her patients in her Green Lake home. Many of the prostitutes whose birthings she assisted came down from the Alaska-Yukon or up from the Seattle waterfront.[5] Some had arranged to place their babies in an orphanage or a children's home following the birth.[5] A few of the mothers offered their babies for adoption, but demand was low. A very small number of women found themselves emotionally distraught after giving birth and decided to keep their babies. Some actually left their profession. Subsequently, they may have restarted their lives with a new profession, claiming to be widowed. A few patients did not divulge their plans for their babies or themselves to Alice. One thing was for sure—every woman was different, and each had her own story and her own plans.

Typically, a mother and her companion, often a lady friend, would show up at the home and ring the doorbell. Pierson was very handy and had installed a twist-style doorbell that would ring in Alice's kitchen and could be heard in her upstairs bedroom at night. Since the women stayed with Alice for up to two weeks, she often got to know them well and learned the stories of their lives.

That June, Alice had a full house. Two healthy mothers from Alaska, Nellie and Cora, and their babies occupied both beds in the front parlor.

A few days later, Nellie and Cora left with their babies. They did not know each other before giving birth at Alice's house. However, they soon became friends. Good friends. They were both from the Midwest; Nellie, from Chicago; and Cora, from Saint Louis. After giving birth, they decided to move in together, like sisters, and keep their babies.

Nellie's baby boy was a funny-looking kid with a small jaw, small head, and small, narrow eyes.[18, 19] Cora's little girl was born bottom down, and her right leg was shorter than her left leg.[18, 19] Both mothers knew they would need help. They devised a plan to help each other with household expenses and childcare. They chose not to return to Alaska but to remain in Seattle. They decided to keep working as prostitutes.

After all, the income was decent.

Doc Brown & Catherine's Birthing Story

In 1896, Doc Brown had suffered an unimaginable tragedy. He lost his first wife, Catherine, and their baby, when she was seven months pregnant, back in New York. Her kidneys had failed.[5] She died in his arms. At that time, he had just finished medical school at Bellevue Medical College and was practicing. Bellevue Medical Center (1736), which was known as the oldest public hospital in the country, had established the first maternity ward (1799) in the United States.[39] He was tormented by this horrendous event. He told Alice that this tragedy was a reminder to him that there were times when medical outcomes were out of his hands, no matter how skilled he was, and that a higher power was in charge. The misfortune transformed him. He committed to God that he would always make time to help those less fortunate than himself, especially women who were expectant with child.

In the early 1900s, there was little or no before-birth care, particularly for women of low social status, such as prostitutes.[24] Doc Brown moved to Seattle in 1898 to answer the call for doctors. There, he met a fine woman named Rose, and they married and had two children. She was expecting their third child.

Helen's Birthing Story

Late one night, the doorbell rang. Alice could see the fear in the eyes of the very young woman standing at the door. She welcomed her in. Her name was Helen. She was pregnant and due to have a baby very soon. She complained of a few false pains that went away when she lay down.[22, 39, 40] Alice normally did not let women stay unless they were ready to give birth, but she made an exception for Helen. Alice sensed that Helen required extra care and perhaps a listening ear.

Helen had joined a dance troupe from Portland, Oregon. The company toured and ventured to Skagway, Alaska, to provide entertainment for the gold miners. Skagway was a launching site and last stop for miners readying to ascend the Chilkoot Pass to the Yukon. Many men took dogsleds on this 600-mile journey.[26] Helen's intention was to stay in Skagway with the troupe for six months. The dance company paid well.

One of the local men in Skagway, Alfred, befriended her. At first, he was caring and polite. However, one night after the show, he invited her to the saloon to have a few drinks. She agreed. She didn't remember much about that night except waking up in his bed the next day. Helen worried about what might have happened. Her mind was a blank. She could not remember a thing. Alcohol did not sit well with Helen. She was ashamed just thinking about what might have occurred.

Illustration 35. Skagway's Broadway on May 20, 1898. Photograph by Eric Hegg, Permission granted from University of Washington, Special Collection, Hegg20A.

It wasn't long before Helen found her self drinking with Alfred again and going to his home. This time, though, it was different. She woke up with a strange man lying next to her and an Eagle (a ten-dollar gold piece) in her shoe. This time, rather than being ashamed, she envisioned a business opportunity. She realized that she had a commodity that was valuable in Skagway, and she could exploit it for money. Good money.

Alfred had lots of friends whom he wanted her to meet. They were both successful. The traveling act returned to Portland, Oregon, but Helen remained in Skagway, which considered itself the true gateway to the Klondike gold fields.

As Alice's house was full the night Helen appeared on her doorstep, Alice made a place for Helen to sleep in the front hall. A few days later, Helen's labor began. A friend named Mavis from the brothel came in to help. Helen's contractions were becoming more frequent, and she would soon give birth.

Helen had prearranged for Doc Brown to attend her birth. Sadly, he had not even examined her. He was hoping to do that this week. So Alice gave Doc a call, and he arrived shortly thereafter.

Meanwhile, Myrtle and Marie had walked over to Pierson and Clara's house for the duration of Helen's confinement. Marie peeked out the window and exclaimed, "Grandma, come look. See that doctor with the big, black bag? I think there is a baby in it." [5]

Pierson and Myrtle looked at each other and started to laugh.

Clara stepped in, saying, "You two, stop it!"

Myrtle put on her big sister shoes and sneered, "Now Marie, you know that babies are born in our house even when the doctor is not there."

Marie shrugged her shoulders and followed her grandma to the kitchen to make bread. Myrtle was such a *smarty-pants,* she thought.

Helen had assisted another woman from the brothel with her birth, and she was relieved to see Doc Brown when he walked through the door. She admired his skill and demeanor with women, including prostitutes. He was very professional and never condescending.

Helen's labor progressed quickly. Her contractions were close together. Doc pulled out a pinard, which was a metal instrument for listening to the baby's heart. It was an instrument that he had brought from New York. He left the pinard at the house.

Doc gave Alice the pinard to listen to the infant's heart through Helen's lower abdomen. He opened the packet that Alice had prepared for the delivery. All of a sudden there was a gush of fluid. It was clear. This was good.

Illustration 36. A pinard or fetoscope.[5]

Then Doc lifted the blanket and saw a tiny hand sticking out, holding a pulsating cord. Not good. There wasn't much time. Alice was listening to the fetal heartbeat. It was strong. She told Doc, and he was satisfied that the baby was stable.

Alice carefully told Helen, "Your baby's cord is protruding and is in the baby's hand. Right now, your baby is doing fine.

Doc is going to make sure the baby's head is tucked down, and he will assist you as you push your baby out. Just like a corkscrew." Luckily, it happened quickly. Helen let out a big moan. She was ready. She pushed, breathing in and out as she did so.

She tore a bit, but the baby came out within twenty minutes. The cord did break in the process. Blood sprayed throughout the room. Quickly, Doc tied off the end of the cord that was attached to the placenta, while Alice tied off the baby's cord. Alice was concerned since there wasn't much cord left on the baby, but she was able to tie it off. The delivery was very quick, and both mom and baby were OK.

Doc proclaimed, "You have a girl."

Right after the birth, Alice placed the baby on the mother's chest and patted her dry.

Doc exclaimed, "Best place for a baby."

Alice grinned; she had trained Doc Brown so well.

The part of the cord that was still attached to the placenta was hanging between Helen's legs, and both Doc and Alice watched for it to descend as the placenta detached. It descended slowly.

The placenta came next, to everyone's relief. Doc gave the placenta to Alice, and she inspected it to make sure that it was not missing any pieces. All was well.

Helen asked Alice to take the baby for a moment while she

gathered her thoughts. She was recovering well. Alice gave the baby to Mavis, who was delighted to help.

Alice invited Doc, Mavis and the new baby to go with her to the kitchen and sample her new blackberry pie.

Shortly after, Alice came back and palpated Helen's abdomen, she was trying to feel the top of the uterus. She could not find it. So Alice removed the pillows behind Helen, so that she could lie flat.

Back in Wisconsin Alice helped Grandma French with birthing and she had warned Alice to never be satisfied **after** a birth unless you know what the uterus is doing – its your duty! If you can't find the uterus, lay the woman flat.

So she did. There it was. Much higher than normal. Not very firm, and over to the right. Then Alice based her thoughts on Grandma French's teachings, which were first see if a mother might need to go to the bathroom.[19]

She preferred the mother to walk to the bathroom. However, Alice decided to bring in the chair Pierson had devised. It normally had a weaved seat, Pierson had removed the seat so the mother could go to the bathroom. Alice placed a pot underneath to collect the urine or any debris. She also started dripping water from a spout of a water container. The tinkling sounds of water dripping encourage the mother to urinate. It worked.

Alice laid Helen back down, and then could feel the top of

the uterus much better; it was still soft, slightly spongy and Alice was concerned, so she proceeded to massage the top of the uterus until it was firm like a coconut.

Now Alice was satisfied.

Doc had finished the pie and excused himself as he left for home.

Mavis reluctantly gave Alice the lovely sleeping baby before she returned to the brothel. Mavis loved newborn babies.

The house was quiet.

Alice laid the baby in a cradle next to Helen's bed. She then went into the kitchen to start cooking. She loved cooking. One of her favorite parts of her business was to be able to provide warm meals for the mothers after their births. They always seamed so grateful and complimentary of her cooking talents.

Alice brought out Helen a warm meal and notice that she was not paying attention to the baby. After Helen had eaten the meal, Alice sat down and explained to Helen that she must feed her baby even if she was not going to be keeping her. She placed the baby in Helen's arms.

Helen seemed to understand.

Alice went over to put more wood in the stove and to boil some more water. When she returned, Helen was teary-eyed.

Helen meekly said, "Alice, I can't do this. I can't have the baby suckle on my chest."

Alice asked her, "Oh my, what is bothering you Helen?"

Helen was silent.

Then the thought came to Alice that the only way Helen had used her body, particularly her chest, prior to this day was for men's—and possibly her own—pleasure. Alice asked her, "What feelings do you have when the baby sucks?"

Helen responded, "I know this is not right. I am so ashamed, but my feelings are sexual. Not for a baby. How can this be? I feel terrible. I am so ashamed. How can a grown woman have such improper feelings?

Now Alice completely understood. She spoke softly. "Helen, these feelings you are having are not necessarily only sexual, but feelings of love. Love that is true. A love that exists between a mother and her baby. Embrace these feelings Helen. Let these feelings grow. These love feelings will allow you to relax and allow your milk to flow to your baby. Every baby needs this, Helen, just like you once did. Give your baby the love she needs. You are her mother. Only you can do this."

Alice decided to leave the room and let Helen spend time getting to know her baby. They needed time to bond. When Alice came back to the front parlor, she saw that Helen had relaxed. It was a beautiful sight—She was nursing her baby. The baby and mother had become attached.

Helen looked up at Alice and softly said, "Her name is Grace, and I love her."

Alice understood.

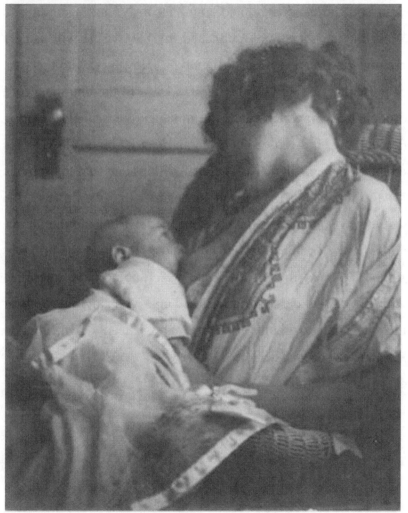

Illustration 37. A mother nursing her baby, early 1900s. Even though this baby is older than a newborn, Helen may have looked something like this. (PacificMotionBirths.com).

Complex presentations, as called in 1880 and such as what occurred in Helen's delivery, can present special problems for the attending physician or midwife.[40] With Helen's delivery, the head and the hand presented simultaneously, and according to W.S. Playfair's textbook published in 1880, "This will usually not give rise to any serious difficulty."[40] However, with this type of presentation, there is a higher incidence of the umbilical cord dropping down, which can result in dangerous sequelae. During descent, the cord can be occluded and restrict blood flow, or the cord can snap off in utero. These conditions can lead to asphyxia for the infant and may result in death.[40] In Helen's case, the delivery was rapid and the cord snapped off outside the uterus, allowing the doctor to tie off both ends. However, the arm was stretched far in front of the head, which could have interfered with the baby's descent during delivery. Yet, time allowed for the physician to gently tuck the baby's head down, chin to sternum, as she was delivered.[40]

Maggie's Birthing Story

One afternoon a few weeks later, a well-to-do young lady of the evening named Maggie came into Alice's home. She had made the trip down from Alaska.[5] She was tall and slender and did not appear to be in need of confinement. She disclosed that she had been cramping all day. Alice was apprehensive, she took her back to the treatment room to examine her, and sure enough, underneath her whalebone corset was a small, protruding belly. There was a heartbeat. Alice confirmed Maggie's fear. Maggie was frightened, as she knew she was not far into her pregnancy. Alice was also frightened. She had to act fast.

Doc Brown was out of town that week and Alice was in need of some extra hands. She heard her daughters, Myrtle and Marie, rattling around in the kitchen.[5]

Myrtle and Marie understood that they needed to go to Grandma Clara's house whenever a woman who was expectant with child came to the house. This was different. They did not think this pretty woman was expecting, so they stayed in the house. Two other women were in the front parlor, lying-in with their new babies.

Alice grabbed the girls and told them that she needed their help. She always knew that someday she would train the girls, but she did not imagine training them at such young ages.[5]

Alice's first command was for Myrtle to boil the water, and

then stand right next to Maggie's head and breathe with her. She sent Marie next door to Grandma's to bring back a big shoebox and a towel. The labor only lasted for thirty minutes. Young Myrtle and Marie were there to help.

Maggie called out the proverbial warning for all, "It's coming!"

Swiftly, Alice crouched down low and caught the baby. The baby was a boy. His breathing was shallow. His color was blue. His body was covered with fine hair and there was not the *white, cheesy substance* she had seen with other early births. His skin was thin and Alice could see his veins. His arms and legs were not flexed and not moving much. He made a slight grimace.[19]

Maggie exclaimed, "I am not staying. I need to go." She did not want to see the baby.

The baby boy was very small. Alice knew this was not good. She gently wrapped him in a towel and laid him in the shoebox.

Maggie was getting restless and wanted to leave soon.

Soon after the placenta was delivered, Alice carefully walked a staggering Maggie out to the front of the house. Alice reminded her to massage her belly when she got back to the brothel. It should be hard, like a coconut, she told her.

Maggie silently nodded.

A young man, perhaps a driver for the Seattle brothel, waited outside in a horse-drawn carriage, ready to whisk Maggie away.

She left as suddenly as she had appeared. Alice stood on her doorstep, watching the carriage grow smaller in the distance.

In a daze, she walked back into the house. Walking past the two women who were feeding their babies in the front parlor, then back to the birthing room, where she found her young daughters tackling a very mature undertaking. Myrtle and Marie were gently drying off the baby and warming him with towels. They had wiped the mucous out of his mouth. They were cushioning him with cotton balls.[5] They placed him back in the shoebox, which they tucked into the cradle next to the potbellied stove where he could stay warm. Myrtle had instructed Marie to go to the parlor to get some breast milk from the two women who had just birthed in the past week. With an eyedropper, they were feeding the baby and gently stroking his cheek.

Alice was stunned and delighted.

Alice originally had intended the shoebox to be a coffin. However, her girls had found a better use. The baby's future was uncertain, but for the moment, he had two special little mamas to take care of him.[5] They named him Samuel.

He would live.

Many women gave birth in Alice's home, and she began to see that she could make it financially and provide for her family. On occasion, a young married woman would ask to birth in Alice's home. Alice would welcome this experience.

One such woman was Mollie.

Mollie & Nick's Birthing Story

Mollie was a married woman who had moved to Seattle from Denver. Her husband was a banker and had received a good offer to move to the Northwest. They did not have family or close friends. They had arrived in Seattle a month earlier and were living in an apartment building with paper-thin walls—not an ideal location to birth.

Early one morning, Mollie rang Alice's doorbell and asked if her husband, Nick, could attend the delivery. Alice had not seen many husbands who wanted to attend a birth, however, she realized he was Mollie's closest friend. Alice agreed. Nick was very kind. They were both young and appeared scared.

Mollie's labor moved slowly. It was off and on for two days. She was experiencing false pains. Finally, after a good night's rest, productive contractions kicked in. Mollie was doing a good job of breathing, and her husband was doing a great job of keeping her calm. However, she started to become uneasy and was losing control.

Alice thought about her own births and how Clara had helped her to relax. She escorted Mollie and her husband into the kitchen. She had Mollie place her hands flat on the table, and like Clara had done with Alice, she gave her some bread dough to knead.

It worked. It kept Mollie focused and gave purpose to her labor. It allowed Nick to stand behind his wife and massage her back. Alice gave Nick a rolling pin.

Alice silently laughed at herself. She had vowed never to have the women she assisted do practical tasks like this one, but it was working. Can't argue with a treatment that works.

The young couple was doing well, and Alice was in the kitchen, where she could boil water to place in the copper pot to warm up the bed. Alice moved Mollie over to the birthing chair.

Pierson had constructed the birthing chair to keep in the kitchen. Clara had noticed that many women liked to use their spinning wheel chairs to assist them to birth, so she asked Pierson to make the birthing chair similar to a spinning wheel chair. It had three legs so the mother could rock. The chair legs were shorter than normal to allow the mother assume a supported squat. The seat was small so the mother could sit on the edge with no pressure on her presenting part. Some mothers sat on the chair backward. Alice placed a large kettle pot under the chair to collect any droppings. The chair could be moved close to the table, on which the mother could rest her arms. Alice called Clara in to assist. Clara was quietly delighted to see Alice being so practical as she assisted Mollie in birth.

Mollie did not say much. She was breathing well. They all knew it was time. Mollie had planned to use the birthing room for the delivery, but the chair was so comfortable and effective that she decided to give birth right there in the kitchen.

Clara brought some blankets and made a nest for her on the kitchen floor.

Mollie eventually got off the chair and moved to the floor. She got on all fours and delivered right there. Nick continued to be part of the birthing process. With a few deep, slow breath in and out, Mollie let out a sigh and was able to push the baby out.

It was a healthy, beautiful boy. He went right to Mollie's chest and soon started suckling. Both Clara and Alice hugged Nick and praised him for being such a big help. If only more fathers would attend the birth with the mothers, they thought.

Illustration 38. A three legged birthing chair.[5]

~*~

Alice had everyone—including Clara, her daughters, and the women who stayed in her home—making pads for the women and infants. They used scraps of flannel to create reusable and washable sanitary pads and diapers.[5] After they made the pads, they were instructed to cut small strips of cheesecloth to darn to the center of the pads or diapers.[22, 39, 40] The cheesecloth would act as a strainer, allowing liquids to pass and collecting solids, such as the mother's blood clots or infant's stool and other debris.[5] The mother could then dispose of the cheesecloth with the solids, rendering the pads and diapers easier to wash.[5]

Alice always placed water on the stove to boil during a women's confinement. She used the boiled water for cleansing and warmth. She poured the water into a copper tin she had received from a German-immigrant midwife she knew in Milwaukee. She placed it between the sheets. Mothers loved crawling into a warm bed after birthing.

Illustration 39. A German-made copper-tin bed warmer .[5]

Stella's Birthing Story

Stella was brash. Stella was hasty. No knock. No doorbell. She barged in without an introduction and made it clear what she was there to do. "I'm here to have a baby," she announced. "Let's make it happen!"

Stella was twenty-six years old and had given birth four times. This was her fifth. Her first baby, who was small, died one week after he was born in San Francisco. Her next two babies arrived very early while she was living in Dawson and died within hours of their births. They were not ready. The fourth baby was born in Seattle and did fine. Stella nursed the baby for a month or two, and then dropped her off at a charity home. That was her plan for this baby, as well.

To Alice's amazement, Stella had been working as a prostitute until just two weeks prior to giving birth. She had arranged with the brothel to work only with men who were very drunk. She laid the drunken men out on the bed and then she did the rest. Stella had it all figured out.

Stella walked back to the treatment room, and when the contractions came, she began huffing and puffing like a locomotive steam train climbing through the Cascades. She was no novice at birthing.

Alice was in the kitchen, listing a few of the birthing options that she offered in her home.

Stella brazenly told Alice, "Don't fret. I don't need no companion, no doc, and if you don't get in here soon, I won't need you."

Alice chuckled. Stella was not a run-of-the-mill woman ready to birth.

With a yelp and a holler, Stella shouted, "Alice, git in here, will ya? Two or three pushes and we will have this baby out."

Alice came in, Stella pushed, and the baby was out. Simple and quick.

The baby was screaming in less than a minute and pinked up quickly.

Alice announced, "You have a boy!"

The large baby boy appeared to be angry, cussing between his grunts and cries.

Already a Klondike man.

He was at least nine pounds and as pink as could be, and he suckled as soon as he was put to Stella's chest.

Stella looked at Alice, and before she even expelled her placenta, she asked, "What's for dinner?"

Alice was amused. She knew this mom would appreciate her home-style cooking and blackberry pie. After she helped her clean up, she walked Stella to the front parlor and helped her get situated in her new bed. She offered to take the baby and lay him in the cradle.

Stella said, "No I'll keep him, he is ready to nurse." Pointing to her bussom, she told Alice, "In my business, I call these my sisters—my own liquid gold. After a month or so of this baby suckling, I will be ready. You see, the milk is part of my Klondike package...Men always like a good drink and a smoke after sex. And if I play my cards right, I won't have the curse for at least a year or two. I will need to work around the clock, seven days a week. But this could bring in some of the gold money, Klondike cash. It happened with my last baby."

Alice was taken aback to hear a woman be so brazen and frank. But this was Stella. Stella told Alice that she would be heading to the Far North again—to Fairbanks, Alaska, this time, since a new gold rush was happening there.[27]

Stella's after-pains were frequent and intense. Alice knew this was common for women who had given birth many times. Alice enjoyed Stella, but was saddened to see that this baby was just a disposable part of Stella's plan to increase her bussom size and milk supply. No baby should be treated this way, Alice thought. It was times like these that led Alice to question her ability to care for women like Stella.

Did Stella sense Alice's disapproval of her wild ways? Stella was kind to the baby, but she lacked the love that Alice had seen between other women and their babies.

Nevertheless, Alice enjoyed Stella's humor and desired to hear Stella's story. As women stayed in Alice's home for up to two weeks after giving birth, she frequently became acquainted with the details of their lives. Alice needed to remind herself that there was no room for judgment in her line of business.

Stella had been raised in San Francisco by her dad—kind of, sort of. Her mother had died of tuberculosis when Stella was six years old. Her father worked in the shipyards when he wasn't out on a bash or drunken spree. Stella was the only girl—she had four brothers. They often had to fend for themselves. They were poor. She dropped out of school at twelve years of age and went to work in the saloons. At first, she cleaned them. However, within a very short time, perhaps a week, she was promoted. She was asked to work as a dance hall girl. She lied about her age. No one cared or questioned her. She had a sweet face. She could not dance. It didn't matter.

In spring 1898, Stella was off to Dawson City in the Yukon at nineteen years of age. She was in the first group of dance hall girls to go to the Far North. She claimed she met Jack London. Stella was remarkably strong and gorgeous. However, when she spoke, she sounded like a man. Her voice was deep and husky, and her words were filthy. She claimed to enjoy life as a prostitute. It was fun and adventurous, and she could make fast cash.

Just before Stella left, Alice contacted Doc Brown to ask him to come by and see Samuel, who was already two weeks old.

When Doc arrived, Alice asked the girls to bring Samuel into the treatment room. Samuel was doing remarkably well. His mamas, Myrtle and Marie, took him to Clara's house every night. Clara helped them with the shift work. They knew this baby needed to be fed frequently.

Alice knew they would be asking Stella to donate some milk. They asked. Stella obliged.

Doc Brown examined Samuel and told the girls, "You girls are angels from heaven. You are part of a great miracle that is happening right here in your home."

The girls beamed with pride. Baby Samuel was well. They took him over to Clara's for the rest of the night. They were excited to tell Grandma the good news.

Doc told Alice that normally for a baby of Samuel's size, he would suggest hospital care—ideally, in a hospital that specialized in the care of sick children and babies. But in 1906, the closest children's hospital was in San Francisco, which, after the great quake, was damaged beyond repair.[37] In lieu of this, the girls were able to administer the most powerful medicines, which were love and constant attention. Baby Samuel was loved like no other child. Doc agreed to stop by in the next few weeks to check on the baby. However, not everyone was fortunate to have positive health outcomes as the girls did with their dear baby Samuel. Both Alice and Doc had seen premature babies perish who were older than Samuel, which was a more common occurrence.

Early Seattle land speculator and real estate developer James Clise and his wife, Anna Clise, watched helplessly as their youngest son, Willis, six, suffered swelling in his joints and bones, and perhaps his heart (his death certificate claimed heart disease[38]), resulting from untreatable "inflammatory rheumatism." [41, 42] He died in 1898. This unfortunate illness led to the formation of the Children's Orthopedic Hospital Association. [41, 42]

In 1907, Anna Clise formed the Children's Orthopedic Hospital Association. She received support from affluent Seattle women, who contributed twenty dollars each, and 105 Seattle citizens, who agreed to buy ten-dollar memberships to the association. They instituted a policy to accept all children regardless of race, religion, gender, or the ability to pay. Then, the association contracted with Seattle General Hospital to rent seven beds per week at for seven dollars each. This enabled the association to offer treatment to its first thirteen patients. Most of the children whom the association treated suffered mainly from orthopedic afflictions of the spine and joints. Some of these afflictions were congenital, such as hip dislocation. Others were acquired, such as rickets, which results from poor nutrition, or paralysis of the spine, hip, or knee, resulting from diseases, such as tuberculosis.[41, 42]

Dr. Casper W. Sharples and eleven other Seattle doctors generously donated medical services to Children's Orthopedic Hospital Association patients.[41, 42]

By 1908, the hospital had moved to a twelve-bed cottage on Queen Anne Hill. Three years later, it moved to a forty-bed, brick building. In 1909, Lillian Carter, a nurse, became the first hospital director. Dr. George McCulloch, the first pediatrician in the West, was recruited. He diversified the types of conditions that could be treated at the hospital.[41, 42]

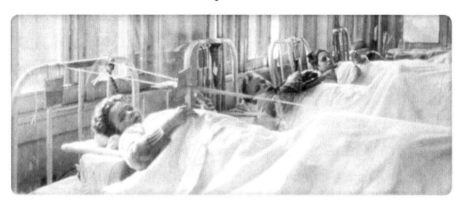

Illustration 40. The First Arrangement. Orthopedic patients receiving care at Seattle General Hospital, 1907. (Courtesy of Seattle Children's Hospital.)

Seattleites loved their children and were saddened to see so many fall ill. They made generous contributions.[41, 42]

~*~

Alice was having an extremely busy summer. Her beds were always full. Everyone was praising Alice's blackberry pie. Myrtle and Marie never had to go beyond the walls of their own home to find milk donors for Samuel. They told Grandma Clara that God knew Samuel needed fresh milk, and he was delivering it on a daily basis. The whole family felt God's grace.

Alice reflected on the fact that the birth of a child was not always a joyful experience, particularly for a prostitute. Yes, the mother was happy to be relieved of the confinement of pregnancy, but not at the reality of bringing forth a new life. Even for the few prostitutes who decided to keep their babies, Alice often saw hesitancy in their attempts to bond with their infants. As the women gazed upon their infants for the first time, Alice wondered if they were trying to decipher who the father was, or if they understood that they would most likely never know.

As years passed, a few of the Klondike prostitutes left the profession and went on to become successful entrepreneur's, or they married prominent citizens. Ray Alderman, one notable red-light woman, married Tom Marquam, the mayor of Fairbanks, Alaska.[27] It was the scandal of the century. It became more heated when Ray hosted a visit from US President Warren Harding.[27]

In its early days, Seattle was a small logging town where men knew that hard work and perseverance could pay off. Then it was transformed into a bustling city of gold miners, speculators, and entrepreneurs, where men dreamed that chance and good luck could provide fast cash.[6, 7] Seattle had became a haven for whiskey, gambling, and wild women.[27]

Prostitution was often glamorized. Many prostitutes achieved monetary success and autonomy, but at what cost? Had they sold more than their bodies? There was a dark, disturbing side to prostitution. Not everyone wanted to talk about it.

Including the prostitutes.

Ella's Birthing Story

Early one incredibly cool morning, Alice heard the doorbell ring. Perhaps it was two in the morning. A tearful woman named Ella stood at the door. Her eyes were blackened, and blood dripped from her mouth where a tooth was missing and a small wound on her cheek. A horse and buggy had brought Ella and a friend named Mamie to Alice's from Madame Ruby's brothel, located near the Seattle waterfront. Alice let them in and seated them in the front room.

Ella could barely speak. Mamie spoke for her. Ella was pregnant. She was not ready for confinement, or so she thought. Like Stella, she planned to work until almost the end of her pregnancy, taking in the most drunken customers.

The night before, Ella had been with a man named Jesse, a gold miner who had just returned to Seattle from Dawson City. Jesse was nearly broke. He had been confident that he would strike it rich, but he didn't. He had joined a group of disgruntled gold miners on the arduous, 600-mile journey down to Skagway, Alaska, where he boarded a ship for Seattle.[27]

When Jesse arrived in Seattle, he decided to take his remaining funds and comfort himself with corn juice and women. After Jesse drowned his sorrows in firewater at the Central Saloon near the waterfront, Chester, the barkeeper, sent him down the road to the brothel to talk to the Calico Queen,

Madame Ruby, an elderly woman who managed the house.

Ruby greeted Jesse at the door and welcomed him in. She wore a dazzling, long, sparkly gown from Asia. She draped her body with glistening beads and bangles. She used henna to redden her hair and cover the gray. Her face was overly powdered and her brows were artificially darkened. She reeked of cheap perfume. All this in an attempt to look younger. She didn't.

Ruby initially was hesitant about Jesse; he was not as drunk as she would have liked him to be. Still, she thought that Jesse would be an easy job for Ella, who was approaching her sixth month of pregnancy. She carried it well. Loose clothing and dark rooms hid her condition.

Ella was called down to escort the drunken and swaggering man upstairs to the end room, called the den. The den was secluded and very dark. It was the most private room in the house. It was not as nice as the "gold mine," the most coveted room in the house, but that room was occupied. On its door was a plaque reading, Come Strike it Rich.

Everything seemed to be going well, or at least Ella believed it was. Then Jesse became belligerent, and in a moment of wild rage, he picked Ella up and threw her against the wall. He muffled her cries for help and knocked her unconscious. Then he had intercourse with her motionless body. He was brutal. He left Ella for dead.

Jesse was packin' iron. He walked down the hall, down the stairs, and over to the front desk, where an oil lantern was burning. Madame Ruby's head was down as she focused on her financial books.

Jesse quietly approached, pulling out his gun. He placed the barrel on Ruby's temple and slapped his other hand over her mouth. He spoke softly. "If you scream, I'll shoot. Don't do it."

Ruby complied.

Jesse had Madame Ruby empty the night's proceeds from the till into his bag. Then slipped out into the wild darkness of the Seattle streets.

Madame Ruby's brothel had been violated. She recognized the robber as the man she had reluctantly sent to Ella. His eyes had been the glazed eyes of a tormentor. Without delay, she called for everyone in the brothel, including the male customers, to search the rooms.

There lay Ella, barely breathing, in a pool of her own blood in the den. Her clothes were torn. Her body was bruised. Her mouth was bloody and a tooth was broken. She had been beaten badly. Her protruding belly was exposed and battered. The brothel shut its doors and the women gathered to tend to Ella. The men left. They understood.

It was events like this that forced the women of the brothel to acknowledge the dark side of their business. Cries of mourning echoed throughout the house.

Madame Ruby didn't know what to do. City authorities were already threatening to close the house. If she called the police or sent Ella to a hospital in town, it would not bode well for the brothel. She pondered this problem as the women cared for Ella.

Ruby did not call the police or the hospital, but she did call the saloon to tell the bartender about Jesse, who was a bad egg. Chester, the barkeep, was contrite.

Three days later, a body was found floating in Elliott Bay. The Seattle police chief's official report said, "A transient man named 'Jesse' had just arrived from Dawson City, Yukon, and had committed suicide." The women at the brothel and the gents at the saloon knew this was not the case. Notably, so did most of the policemen.

Ella was bloody and dazed. They hoped she would live. The women assisted in cleaning her up. Two hours later, at one o'clock in the morning, Ella had faint, irregular contractions, and her stomach became semi-rigid and painful. Madame Ruby knew that Alice could help. She called a driver to bring a buggy for Ella and requested that one of the women accompany her. Mamie volunteered to go. They bundled up with a wool blanket and rode to Alice's house. Madame Ruby knew Alice would provide good care.

Alice and Mamie took Ella back to the treatment room. Ella could not feel the baby move. Her belly was painful and rigid to the touch. The dark bleeding had stopped.[19] So had the contractions. Alice listened with the pinard and could not hear a fetal heartbeat. So Alice made a bed for Ella in the front parlor and encouraged her to get sleep. Mamie had a vial of opium that Ruby had given her to ease Ella's pain. She would need to be rested for the birth. Alice told Mamie that she would check Ella in the morning, but she left a small brass bell to ring, just in case.

A young woman and a baby who would be leaving the next day occupied the other bed in the front parlor. Mamie slept on a small bed-couch in the foyer.

Ella slept almost nonstop for the next two days. She wasn't hungry. Alice heard her moaning with sorrow. Her pain had eased. Ella knew the awful fate that lay ahead for the baby. She ate a little food and took a few sips of water. She healed. The baby never moved.

Mamie stayed.

Alice called in Doc Brown to confirm her suspicion and offer his advice on how the labor should progress. He confirmed that Ella's water had broken and that there was no fetal heartbeat. Like Alice, he felt that Ella needed sleep and chose not to induce labor -just yet. He was concerned about infection, but he thought it would be best if labor started on its own, rather than being induced with ergot. He left Alice's home shaking his head in despair.

On the second night, Alice arose at five o'clock in the morning, and sure enough, Ella was beginning to feel contractions.

Mamie helped Alice move her to the birthing room. In the corner of the room was a small bed.

Ella slowly gravitated to the bed.

Within a few hours, a lifeless, snow-white baby girl was born. The little blood left in her body had pooled in her lips and she looked like a porcelain doll. The baby weighed nearly five pounds and was more developed than they anticipated. After the baby was born, out came the placenta with what appeared to be a large blood clot attached.[5] Alice saved the placenta for Doc Brown to inspect.

Ella knew that the evil man had killed her baby.

Mamie comforted Ella while Alice tended to the baby and prepared her for viewing. Sadly, the baby's skin was already peeling off.[5]

Alice dressed the baby in a small, white dress decorated with tiny, embroidered flowers and wrapped her in a blanket. This was Ella's baby, her first. Ella was tearful and despondent. She wanted to hold the baby—her child.

Alice and Mamie went to the kitchen to allow Ella some time to say good-bye to her little one.

Ella named her Annie, which had been her mother's name. Ella had never known her mother.

Alice called her father to pick up the deceased baby. No one knew where he would take the baby to lay her to rest. No one asked. Pierson did not share.

Life is dreadful.

Doc Brown and Alice estimated that Ella was seven to eight months pregnant at the time of Annie's birth. Ella's breasts became engorged with milk. When she heard about Samuel, her heart listened; she became Myrtle and Marie's best supplier. Ella stayed for a few extra weeks to heal and, more importantly, to supply the girls with milk for Samuel. Everyone was grateful for her generosity during this harrowing time.

~*~

Alice was assisting women who were engaging in high-risk behaviors, which made them vulnerable to the perils of disease. She had heard the Semmelweis story in nursing school as well as from Doc.[34]

In 1846, Ignatz Semmelweis, a young intern in the obstetric clinic in Vienna, Austria, noticed that the local midwives' clinic had a 1.5 percent mortality rate, whereas the medical students' clinic had a 15 percent mortality rate. The midwives taunted the medical students about the disparity.[34]

Then, one of Semmelweis's colleagues infected his finger during a postmortem and succumbed to sepsis. Semmelweis was outraged at the neglect of cleanliness. He then realized that medical students were attending autopsies in the morgue and then traveling to the confinement room.

Immediately, he required that students wash their hands with chlorine water after the autopsies and before attending to the pregnant women. Miraculously, mortality rate at the medical students' obstetric clinic plummeted below that of the midwives' clinic.[34]

Communication, particularly transatlantic, was weak and it took many years to disseminate Semmelweis's research to American medical and obstetric practices.

Alice strove to keep her dwelling warm and inviting, while maintaining stringent standards of cleanliness. She adopted scrupulous hand-washing and other sanitation methods in order to prevent the transmission of infectious disease to women and their infants during birth.[34]

A mutual admiration between Alice and the prostitutes existed. She respected them and offered them decent care.

They understood each other.

Illustration 41. Johns Hopkins Hospital, 1900. (National Archives.)

"I never let my schooling interfere with my education."
~Mark Twain

7

1904~Midwifing, Doctoring, & Nursing

Educating and Regulating Providers

Times were changing. Immigrants were streaming in from all over the globe to America. Some came by choice; others, by force. They were by nature somewhat independent and rebellious, seeking opportunity and a chance to live on their own terms. As the westward expansion transpired, law and order became necessary in new settlements. Would the days of the Wild West soon be gone?

The Woods, like thousands of other American families, took part in the westward expansion. As immigrants from northern Europe, their ancestors had helped to colonize the East. Settling in cabins in New York, they soon found themselves fighting their fathers in the Revolutionary War.[5] They reveled in victory and settled into the comfort of their homes. Shortly after, they found themselves fighting with brothers in a bloody Civil War, which gave birth to a modern, industrialized nation and ended slavery, although at a terrible cost.[5] They loaded up their wagons and moved west to the Wisconsin Territory. This time, some fought within their own homes and families, and boarded trains to move to the West—to Seattle, where once again, they settled and began to build a new life.

The Wood family was a microcosm of the nation. All of this happened in less than 120 years. Babies were born, illnesses spread, injuries happened, and deaths occurred. Schools were created and laws were enacted. Americans, rebellious by nature, did not want to be told what to do.

But they *were* told.

In America during the 1800s, the level of education and standards of practice among physicians, midwives, and nurses were varied and unregulated. Education laws and practice standards were often established at the state or local levels, rather than nationwide.[15, 23]

T. Gaillard Thomas, MD, professor of obstetrics at the College of Physicians and Surgeons in New York, had studied obstetrics in Europe. In the late 1800s, he brought back a textbook for his American colleagues and students. The book was titled, *A Treatise on the Science and Practice of Midwifery.*[40] This text was a 600-page obstetric-practice book written by William Playfair, MD, a professor of obstetric medicine at Kings' College in Edinburgh, Scotland.[40] A special edition was published in Thomas's honor for American physicians, and it focused on anatomy, pathophysiology, puerperal disease, and puerperal insanity. The illustrations were useful. The explicit case studies helped to guide physicians with obstetric practices.[40]

Physician Organization, Education, and Standards of Practice

In 1847, Nathan Davis founded the American Medical Association in Philadelphia, Pennsylvania. In 1897, Andrew Taylor Still of Kirksville, Missouri, founded the American Osteopathic Association.[44, 45] In 1900, medical schools varied from elite universities, such as Harvard, Yale, and Johns Hopkins, to commercial medical colleges, often referred to as diploma mills. In 1903, an AMA first section meeting on Obstetrics and Diseases of Women. [15, 44, 45]

In 1904, the American Medical Association (AMA) established a council on medical education with a mandate to investigate and elevate the standards for medical education. The AMA council's first act was to require four years of high school education as a prerequisite for admittance to medical school, and for medical schools to extend the duration of their programs from as little as four months to a respectable four years. In addition, individual state boards declared that medical schools must extend the academic year from four months to eight or nine months, which caused financial hardship for many medical students. The AMA investigation revealed severe discrepancies in the standards of medical schools within the association. It decided not to release the findings, lest they create "ill will," but rather to invite an outside group to review the findings.[15]

The Carnegie Foundation was selected to investigate the education of physicians in America. In 1910, Abraham Flexner, an American educator who trained at Johns Hopkins, examined over 150 medical schools. He then issued the Flexner Report, which uncovered the substandard training of many physicians practicing in America. One of the biggest discrepancies he discovered was that while medical science had advanced, medical education lagged behind. His findings exposed schools that made many false claims. Some flaunted laboratories that were nowhere to be found or consisted of a few test tubes stuffed into a cigar box. Some boasted of libraries that in reality held no books, while others neglected disinfectant use in the dissection rooms, which consequently reeked. Further, Flexner discovered that admittance to medical school was sometimes based solely on a student's ability to pay the tuition. Flexner reported that obstetric education was at the lowest level, where most classes were taught in clinics rather than in hospitals or classrooms. Many medical colleges and physicians challenged the findings of the Flexner Report. Nevertheless, the Flexner Report led to a major reformation of medical education in America.[15]

Physician Obstetric Specialties

In the early 1900s in America, the field of obstetrics was emerging. Typically, general practitioners provided maternal care. Two of the most notable early twentieth-century obstetric pioneers were J. Whitridge Williams and Joseph B. DeLee.[15]

Dr. Williams was a professor at Johns Hopkins and noted for his efforts to raise the standards of obstetrics in American medical schools. He authored *Williams Obstetrics*, a textbook for medical students. Subsequent editions of *Williams Obstetrics* are still being used in the twenty-first century by US medical students.[15]

Dr. DeLee founded the Chicago Lying-In Hospital and was a proponent of keeping maternity hospitals separate from other hospital wards to prevent easy transmission of infection. He encouraged nurses to consider obstetrics as a specialty. He wrote several editions of a textbook called *Obstetrics for Nurses*.[22] He also recommended his book for medical students.

Both men advocated for physicians and/or nurses to specialize in the study of obstetrics.[15, 22]

These pioneer obstetricians introduced many innovative ideas and interventions to diagnose and treat abnormal obstetric events, such as preeclampsia, and to raise the standards of obstetric practice.[15, 33]

Early efforts to organize obstetric societies were at a local level (Boston, 1861; New York, 1863; Philadelphia, 1868; Cincinnati, 1876; and Chicago, 1878). National and regional obstetrical societies soon formed (*American Gynecological Society*, 1876; *American Association of Obstetricians and Gynecologists*, 1888; *Central Association of Obstetrics and Gynecology*, 1929). The *Central Association of Obstetrics and Gynecology* became a national association in 1950. Then a merge between the *National Federation of Obstetric Societies* and the *American Committee on Maternal Welfare* resulted in the *American Academy of Obstetrics and Gynecology* on June 13, 1951. Shortly after, the name changed to the current *American College of Obstetricians and Gynecologists* or *ACOG*, on May 11, 1956. [15, 45]

Physician Pediatric Specialties

The medical specialty of pediatrics arose from the public health movement of the late nineteenth century and served as a model of preventive medicine.[15, 47] Mothers were becoming increasingly concerned about how to protect their children from the perils of disease, such as whooping cough and polio.[15, 47] In 1929, during the Diseases of Children program, an AMA section meeting, in Portland, Oregon, a group of physicians identified a need for a society of pediatricians. In 1930, the American Academy of Pediatrics (AAP) was incorporated.[47]

Midwifery Education and Practice

Early attempts to regulate midwifery practice were often made at a local level, such as in 1716 when New York City required midwives to become licensed. [48]

In the late 1800s, most of the trained midwives practicing in the United States were recent immigrants, and their training varied. At the high end of the training scale, midwives from Sweden and Italy were required to have delivered over one hundred live births under supervion.[23] Many midwives had far less experience. As a result, in the Midwest, midwifery schools were being opened. For example, the Wisconsin College of Midwifery, a German-based program supported by physicians, was established in 1895. Regardless of this initial push to regulate, most women offering midwifery care did not possess credentials of any kind. In Saint Louis in 1894, of the 303 midwives listed in the directory, only twenty-six had any type of credentials, American or European.[23]

As the twentieth century progressed, the relationship between midwives and physicians deteriorated. A "midwife debate" grew. Many midwifery groups considered Dr. Williams and Dr. DeLee to be twentieth-century "titans" who had convinced American society that midwives were untrained and incapable of assisting with birth, and that pregnancy was a dangerous pathological condition for which only specialists could provide care.[23] Indeed, many midwives were not formally or even properly trained. But this was also somewhat true of physicians, though educational reforms in medicine were making it less so. The debate drew national attention to the importance of proper training.[15, 23]

Midwifery schools were established at a slower rate than medical and nursing schools in the United States, however, and it was common practice for male doctors to teach nurses or midwives in the classrooms.[15]

In Utah, a few Mormon (Church of Jesus Christ of Latter-Day Saints) women were sent to Eastern medical colleges. Brigham Young challenged women to become doctors in 1873 and to return to Salt Lake City to offer care for women and to educate the community about birthing. Ellis Reynolds Shipp answered this call, and in 1875 traveled to Philadelphia to attend Woman's Medical College of Pennsylvania. During her second year of medical school, she became pregnant. However, she did not miss one day of school. In May 1877, she passed her exams and the very next day gave birth to a baby girl. She graduated with honors in medicine in 1878 and returned to teach and train midwives, nurses, and doctors.[49-51] During her years as an educator, Dr. Shipp was often pregnant or had a baby in her arms. She gave birth to ten children. Dr. Shipp and the Latter Day Saint Relief Society opened the School of Obstetrics and Nursing and trained over 500 women to become licensed midwives.[23, 49-51]

In 1917, the Washington State legislature passed a statute requiring direct-entry (no prior post-secondary education required) midwives to have two years of schooling. Since the state did not have any midwifery training programs, these regulations applied to midwives trained in the Midwest and the East, as well as those trained in Asia or Europe. The number of practicing midwives dwindled during the 1940s as birthing moved to the hospitals. There was a revival of midwifery in the 1970s, and the Seattle Midwifery School was established in 1978. In 2010, it merged with Bastyr University.[23]

To practice in Washington today in the twenty-first century, caregivers must complete a state-approved educational program to become licensed midwives (LM) and meet a set of standards to become certified professional midwives (CPM) by the North American Registry of Midwives. The Midwives Association of Washington State (MAWS) is a nonprofit, professional organization. It offers a full, professional membership for Licensed Midwives and Certified Nurse Midwives.[48]

Nurse-Midwifery Education

In 1925 there were only two ways to secure qualified nurse-midwives in America. One was by sending American nurses for graduate training in Britain; the other was by recruiting British trained midwives to practice in the United States. In 1932, the Maternity Center Association of New York started the first nurse-midwifery education program. Candidates were often public health nurses. Mary Breckenridge started the Frontier Graduate School of Midwifery in 1939 as a means to serve rural mothers and children in Kentucky. The concept of nurse midwifery on American soil had emerged. [23, 52, 53, 54]

Today, the American College of Nurse Midwives (ACNM), which was incorporated in 1955, serves as a professional organization for Certified Nurse-Midwives as well as Certified Midwives.[53, 54] Today, Certified Nurse-midwives exemplify the call for the United States to increase use of mid-level providers and are often recognized as national leaders serving women and the general public in the US.[23, 53, 54]

Obstetric Nursing Education and Practice

In 1911 the American Nurses Association was formed, and not one of the attendees was a registered nurse, since there were no laws at that time to license nurses.[55] Specialty nursing associations followed.

In 1969, obstetric nurses formed an association within the American College of Obstetrics and Gynecology called the Nurses Association of the American College of Obstetrics and Gynecology (NAACOG). Members sought to improve practices and raise standards for nurses who specialized in women's health, obstetric care, and neonatal care. In 1993, the Association of Women's Health, Obstetric, and Neonatal Nurses, or AWHONN was recognized as an independent association.[56]

American Pharmacists' Education and Practice

American pharmacists were one of the earliest medical-based groups to organize. Their association, known as the American Pharmaceutical Association, was founded in 1852. Nearly every formal pharmacy group can trace its roots to this organization. This group continues to lead the profession of pharmacy, as it has for over 150 years.[57]

~*~

Pregnancy, Birthing, and Infant Care

Two books published in the early 1900s illuminate birthing practices of the era in the home and in hospitals.[22, 43] Dr. W. Lewis Howe's a 1903 treatise, *Care of the Expectant Mother*, gave the expectant mother a "common sense footing as to her condition," preparing her for pregnancy, the birthing process, and the postnatal period, as well as for caring for the child until adolescence. The book was not officially published until 1918. The main premise of this book was that a doctor would be delivering the baby in the woman's home.[35] The second book, Dr. DeLee's *Obstetrics for Nurses* (1904) was intended to educate nurses and medical students about birthing care in the hospital. This book included detailed drawings and photographs taken by Dr. DeLee in the Chicago Lying-In Hospital.[22]

A TREATISE

ON THE

CARE OF THE EXPECTANT MOTHER

DURING

PREGNANCY AND CHILDBIRTH

AND

Care of the Child from Birth Until Puberty

BY

W. LEWIS HOWE, M.D.

PHILADELPHIA
F. A. DAVIS COMPANY, PUBLISHERS
1918

Illustration 42. Book used by expectant women to prepare for a doctor-assisted birth at home. Copyright: 1903. Published 1918. [5, 43]

In his book, Dr. Howe instructs the expectant mother and/or a birth attendant to prepare for confinement (birthing) by securing and preparing a list of supplies.[22]

To prepare the home prior to confinement, women were expected to sprinkle 1 percent carbolic acid on wrapping paper or sheets to protect the floor.[43] He encouraged the use of cheesecloth, as a strainer of debris, with cloth or paper underneath to protect the bed or couch. If possible, the woman was encouraged to deliver on a raised couch. After giving birth, she would be transferred to her bed, which was warmed with hot-water bottles.[43]

Articles Necessary for Childbirth[43]

1. Two cheesecloth and absorbent-cotton bed protectors, one yard square and two inches thick.

2. Four cheesecloth pads twenty-seven inches by eighteen inches, folded and filled with cotton to three inches thick for the first two days after birth

3. Twenty-four pads twenty-one inches by eighteen inches, folded in half.

4. Four dozen six-inch-square pieces of cheesecloth.

These were to be baked in the oven for thirty minutes each day for three days. The pads might become slightly brown.

Wrap them up. The intention is to disinfect everything that comes in contact with the mother. Do not open them until they must be used.

5. A rubber sheet, one yard by two yards.

6. Six to eight large sheets of heavy brown wrapping paper.

7. One bed pan.

8. A four-quart fountain syringe.

9. A bottle of colored corrosive-subliminate tablets (a mercury-based substance thought to be a powerful antiseptic).

10. One-half pound of Squibb's ether (ether is flammable).

11. Safety pins, large and small.

12. Eight ounces of pure olive oil.

13. An eight-ounce package of absorbent cotton.

14. Two yards of unbleached cotton cloth for binder.

15. Four ounces of 3 percent solution of boric acid (for the baby's cord).

At the time of confinement, Dr. Howe suggests using two gallons of water, boiled for thirty minutes and cooled, to wash the external genitalia. He also advises having on hand more boiling water, castile soap, towels, porcelain basins and pitchers, two to three ounces of strained vinegar, and ice. The mother should not be allowed to lift the baby for ten days. Breast-feeding is highly recommended, he says; it is the mother's duty. He suggests that the mother start feeding her baby six to twelve hours after birth, and every five hours thereafter. He encourages mothers to start proper bowel and bladder training for their infants at three months of age by having them sit on the chamber pot four times a day. The goal is to have the baby potty-trained by twelve months of age.[43]

**Expectant mothers: Please contact your provider. The practices described here may harm you or your baby.

In Dr. DeLee's book also encourages breast-feeding, saying it is a mother's duty.[22] He describes simple engorgement as a common disorder. If left alone, it will gradually disappear. Mothers can massage the breasts or use a breast pump, ice, and a breast binder to decrease discomfort. Dr. DeLee describes first milk as indigestible and cathartic in nature.[22] He reminds women that there is no such thing as "milk-fever," and if fever presents, there is an infection. He suggests applying boric acid to the breast, which seems potentially harmful and irritating to the skin, but some infections may have presented a greater threat than that.[22]

**Expectant mothers: Please contact your provider. The practices described here may harm you or your baby.

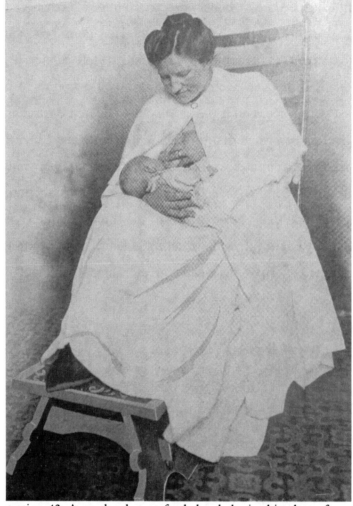

Illustration 43. A mother breast-feeds her baby in this photo from Dr. DeLee's *Obstetrics for Nurses*, published in 1904.[5] He recommends using a rocking chair without arms and a step stool to elevate the leg.

**Expectant mothers: Please contact your provider. The practices described here may harm you or your baby.

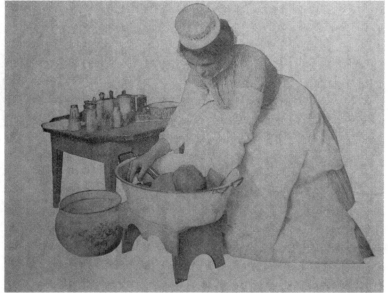

Illustration 44. Dr. DeLee describes how to bathe a baby in *Obstetrics for Nurses*. 1904. [5]

The newborn bath consisted of a daily sponge wash of the face and head with warm water and small amounts of castile soap. Then the body was gently rubbed with benzoinated lard (an ointment with 1percent benzoin) to keep the infant "sweet and clean." Dr. DeLee recommended Albolene cream (an oily white substance made from petroleum) for removing white secretions in the labial folds. Infants were not to be given a full bath until the cord fell off.[22]

**Expectant mothers: Please contact your provider. The practices described here may harm you or your baby.

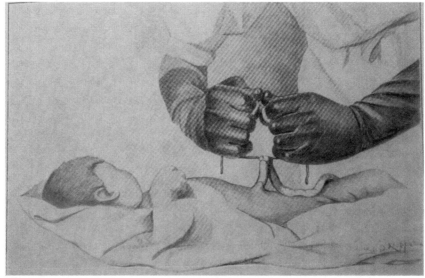

Illustration 45. Tying the cord, as shown in Dr. DeLee's
Obstetrics for Nurses, 1904. In the 1900s, midwives, nurses, and
doctors often used string to tie off the cord. [5]

The cord was tied off with string or thread. A dressing was
applied to the cord. If the cord was moist, Dr. DeLee advised
washing it with 95 percent alcohol.[22]

To encourage a clean environment for infants and mothers
in the lying-in rooms, whether in homes or hospitals, Dr.
DeLee recommended using newspapers, fresh from the press,
as a clean medium with which to collect maternal and infant
debris. Soiled newspapers could be conveniently discarded to
the burn pile.[22]

**Expectant mothers: Please contact your provider. The
practices described here may harm you or your baby.

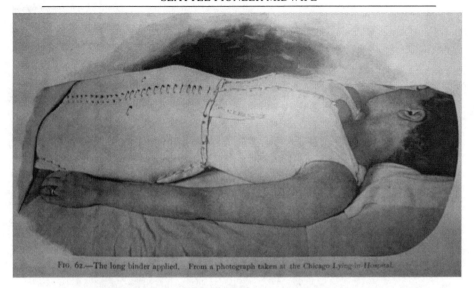

Fig. 62.—The long binder applied. From a photograph taken at the Chicago Lying-in-Hospital.

Illustration 46. In the 1900s, many women requested a binder, as shown in Dr. DeLee's *Obstetrics for Nurses, 1904*, after giving birth.[5]

In the 1900s, many women wore full-length binders after giving birth. During the Victorian and Edwardian eras, binders were understood to preserve women's figures. Women's disappointment in the bodily changes wrought by pregnancy has a long history. Even during Roman times, women had abortions performed to prevent the disfigurement of childbirth.

Dr. DeLee wrote, "Certain changes in the body are the necessary results of child-birth and beautify the figure, although some women do not look at it in this light." [22]

**Expectant mothers: Please contact your provider. The practices described here may harm you or your baby.

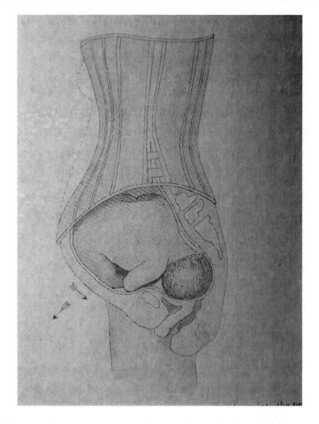

Illustration 47. A pregnancy corset as shown in Dr. DeLee's *Obstetrics for Nurses.* 1904. [5, 22]

A combination of Victorian, Edwardian, and American culture and emerging but tenuous science led some doctors to make the dubious recommendation that mothers should wear a special corset during pregnancy "to help the abdominal wall to carry the weight of the child." [22]

**Expectant mothers: Please contact your provider. The practices described here may harm you or your baby.

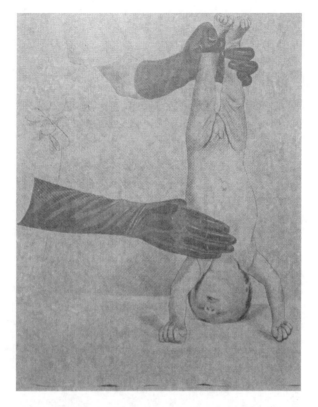

Illustration 48. Newborn resuscitation. Dr. DeLee's *Obstetrics for Nurses* *1904.* [5, 22] shows the standard upside-down procedure.

To resuscitate a newborn, Dr. DeLee wrote, "The child is supported by the feet, with forehead resting on the table, so the head is pressed a little backward. Mucous, blood etc., are removed from the fauces the nurse makes light compression." [22]

**Expectant mothers: Please contact your provider. The practices described here may harm you or your baby.

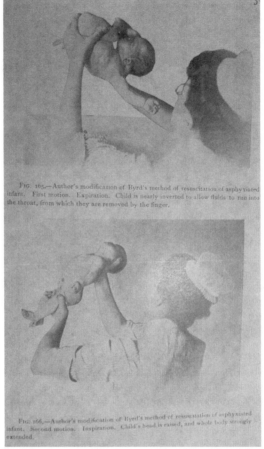

Illustration 50. Newborn resuscitation. The "Byrd" method, as shown in Dr. DeLee's *Obstetrics for Nurses*. 1904.[5, 22]

The other resuscitation maneuver was the Byrd method, which consists of "alternately folding and unfolding the child like a book." [22]

**Expectant mothers: Please contact your provider. The practices described here may harm you or your baby.

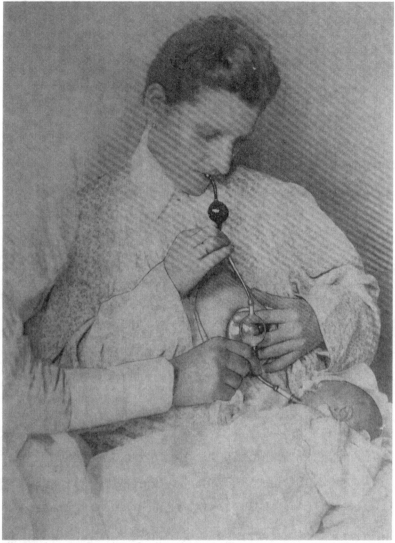

Illustration 51. Mother feeding breastmilk to a premature infant. Dr. DeLee's *Obstetrics for Nurses*. 1904.[5, 22]

**Expectant mothers: Please contact your provider. The practices described here may harm you or your baby.

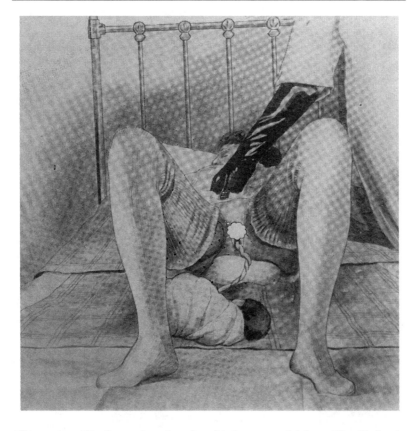

Illustration 52. Preparing for the third stage of labor. Dr. DeLee's *Obstetrics for Nurses*.1904. [5, 22]

Notice the stockings on the women's legs and that the baby was left with the cord attached until the placenta was expelled.[22] In the United States, nurses were instructed to locate the "firm coconut" of the uterus after birth. In the United Kingdom, it was referred to as a "cricket ball." [22, 40]

**Expectant mothers: Please contact your provider. The practices described here may harm you or your baby

During the early part of the twentieth century, puerperal infection was one of the primary causes of infant mortality. Thousands of babies died during childbirth. Even more died in the first four weeks of life from communicable diseases or diseases acquired from contaminated food or water supplies. Eventually, sand filtration improved the water supply, decreasing the incidence of diseases such as typhoid. Regulation of milk improved the milk supply.[15] In 1910, the National Association for the Study and Prevention of Infant Mortality was formed, leading to a sharp increase in the availability of community-based clinics. By 1915, there were 538 baby clinics in America.[15, 58]

According to the Illinois Department of Health, the infant mortality rate in Chicago was 59.6 deaths per 1,000 in 1930, compared to the all-time high of 154.3 deaths per 1,000 deliveries in 1908. Infant mortality drastically declined to 7.8 deaths per 1,000 in 2002.[58]

Water Front. Seattle, Wash.

Property of MSCUA, University of Washington

Illustration 53. The Seattle waterfront in 1907. Permission granted from University of Washington, Special Collections, UW28040.

"If you tell the truth, you don't have to remember anything."
~Mark Twain

8

1907~Unexpected Visitors

The Truth Revealed

The population of Seattle was rapidly growing. In 1870, Seattle was considered a small town of 1,107. Two decades later in 1890, it had expanded to a bustling city of 42,837. Over the next decade, the population nearly doubled to 80,671. By 1910, that number had tripled and the city reported a population of 237,194.[59] Seattle's rapid, uninhibited growth led to vibrant neighborhoods of immense prosperity. However, it also resulted in unforeseen sequelae of unsanitary health conditions.[6]

In the late 1890s, Seattle recognized the need to redevelop its geographical base and port to facilitate receiving and transporting goods and people.[6] The city of Tacoma and its port were better situated geographically than Seattle was, and railroad and shipping companies were viewing Tacoma as a major port in the Puget Sound.[6] This motivated Seattle authorities to redesign the city.

Seattle had completed the first phase of the Denny Hill regrade, in which substantial quantities of dirt were washed into the tidelands of Elliot Bay and the mouth of the Duwamish River.[60-61] This allowed the port of Seattle to be developed to accommodate ships from Asia and the Alaska-Yukon territories. Business was good.[6, 59]

Seattle's Great Fire in 1889 had destroyed all wooden structures in the city. City leaders decided to rebuild using brick and stone, and to construct new buildings one to two stories above the original ground level.[59] This led to the Seattle's underground. Many of the brothels and saloons were located near the Seattle waterfront, Pioneer Square, and the Seattle Underground, which was a collection of underground walkways and rooms.[50, 61] The city was prospering, and ships had easier access to Seattle. Unfortunately, when the ships docked, so did the rats.[60] The rats were unexpected and unwelcome.

In October 1907, a few residents of downtown Seattle developed a sudden fever, chills, enlarged lymph nodes, and necrosis on their bodies. Death followed soon after.[60, 61] Could it be the bubonic plague, the notorious Black Death of the Middle Ages?

The plague, endemic in China for half of the previous century, had jumped to Hong Kong in 1894. Much of the shipping destined for American West Coast ports originated in Hong Kong. At the turn of the century, infected rats and fleas had caused a similar outbreak in San Francisco, killing more than one hundred people.[60]

Seattle health authorities needed to respond to this plague threat covertly. They wanted to prevent panic and avoid any negative publicity with an upcoming world's fair. [5]

Alice had developed a good reputation in the Seattle medical community, and the brothel community trusted her. On average, doctors would stop by twice a week to witness her good care. On one occasion, Doc Brown picked Alice up and took her to a logging site where an accident had occurred.[5] Together, they successfully amputated a lumberjack's leg.[5] In 1903, Pierson had injured his leg. A sawbones looked at the open wound and suggested amputation. Pierson refused. Clara and Alice took charge. They packed the leg with a homemade salve that contained a secret ingredient: very hot cow manure.[5] Miraculously, the leg healed. Alice and Clara joked that not even the bad bugs liked the stench and heat of manure.

So when authorities suspected that people were dying of a medieval curse, both the doctors and prostitutes of Seattle thought of Alice.[5] They demanded that she be brought to the city center.[5] Their demand was met.

City officials sent a horse-drawn carriage to Alice's front door in Green Lake.[5] She immediately sent Myrtle and Marie next door. Alice was informed by the health authorities that the situation was dire and they needed her expertise.[5] The city had sent two women to take care of any women lying-in at Alice's house, but their services were unnecessary. Alice closed shop.

Doc Brown knew that Alice had trained in Milwaukee, another waterfront town, and she had been taught how to care for people with bubonic plague. Alice examined the patients and confirmed their suspicions. It was bubonic plague.[5, 62, 63]

Bubonic plague spreads when fleas that acquire the bacteria from an infected rodent bite people. The person's lymph nodes become enlarged and form "bubos." Sudden fever, chills, and pain in the groin or armpits may precede the swelling. Without treatment, over 50 percent of patients die.[62, 63]

Property of MSCUA, University of Washington Libraries. Photo Coll 273

Illustration 54. Hotel Washington during the Denny Hill regrade in 1907. Permission granted from University of Washington, Special Collections, Warner242.

Immediately, city authorities decided to set up a makeshift hospital next to the Seattle underground. It would be quarantined.[5] On a hunch, they brought out their silver compounds. Americans commonly used colloidal silver to fight off infections in the early 1900s.[64]

Greeks, Romans, and Egyptians had used silver and silver products for centuries, storing all of their unpreserved food in silver containers. During the 1800s, it was a common practice in the United States to store wine, vinegar, and milk in silver containers. People commonly dropped silver coins into milk to prevent it from spoiling prior to the discovery of refrigeration.[64]

Dr. William Halstead, the first chief surgeon of Johns Hopkins Medical School, used silver wire and foil to prevent infections in surgery.[64] Silver nitrate was often administered in newborns' eyes as a prophylactic measure to prevent conjunctivitis, a devastating effect of gonorrhea.[21, 30] Silver was thought to be lethal to bacteria. This was common medical knowledge in the late 1800s and early 1900s, and often used in the care of war casualties.[64] Unfortunately, unmanaged silver treatment could be toxic and posed a threat to the health of the recipient. In other words, do not try this at home.

~*~

The first man with bubonic plague whom they cared for died.[5, 62] A few more patients came in looking to die. There were successes as well as failures. Alice herself was quarantined and could not go home for a week.[5] City authorities demanded secrecy.[5] The city of Seattle was preparing to launch a spectacular world's fair, and the news of people dying from a medieval disease could be disastrous. It could cause a panic.[5, 62]

As feared, the news leaked out; rumors flooded the community. Seattle residents pleaded with the state governor to take charge of this disastrous event. Public Health Services responded and discovered that more than 15,000 rats infested with infected fleas were living in the sewers of Seattle.[62]

~*~

Bubonic plague wasn't the only curse that ships brought to the waterfront in Seattle. Naval ships carried soldiers from around the world, and they brought ailments as well as fortunes and despair as well as hope. Many were welcomed and some were not.[5]

December 16, 1907, was a warm and cloudy day on the Eastern Seaboard of America, President Theodore Roosevelt set out to boast to the world of America's military might by sending out a mighty armada. The US Atlantic Fleet was ordered to tour the world.[65-67] Later to become known as the Great White Fleet, it was a fleet of sixteen steam-powered battleships, all painted white. They would circumnavigate the world in fourteen months. Over 14,000 sailors were aboard these ships. The tour included twenty ports of call on six continents, traveling more than 14,000 miles.

San Francisco was the last port of call in North America for the entire fleet, prior to crossing the Pacific Ocean. On May 6, 1908, Rear Admiral Thomas ordered a few ships to head north to Seattle. They would then return to rejoin the fleet when it departed for the Far East via Australia. The battleship USS *Kansas* was one of the ships that headed to Puget Sound.[65-67]

On May 23, 1908, the *Kansas* made a stop in Seattle.[63] Seattle welcomed the sailors with theater and streetcar tickets. A parade on Seattle's Second Avenue celebrated the arrival of the ships from the Great White Fleet.[66] Onboard the ship was another unexpected guest.

Illustration 55. A postcard of the USS *Kansas*, painted white.[5]

In Green Lake, Alice's home was quiet. Alice had no patients at the house and was taking time to catch up on some spring-cleaning. Marie, now eight years old, opened the door and yelled to her mother, "Mama, there is a big solider man at the door." [65] Alice walked to the door and froze. The blood in her veins boiled. Quickly, she told Marie to go next door to Grandma Clara's and fetch Myrtle, age ten.

It was Gideon, her ex-husband. Immediately, Alice confirmed that he was there on good terms. He explained that he just wanted to have an amiable visit and take Alice and the girls on a tour of the ship. Alice agreed, on the condition that under no circumstances would Gideon would reveal to the girls that he was their father. She felt it would be unfair for them to meet him without warning.[5] He agreed to Alice's terms.

Myrtle and Marie soon returned to the house to meet their mother's old friend. Then, they all went down to the waterfront to tour the ship. Gideon introduced the shipmates to the girls. He told everyone, in front of the little girls, of course, that Alice was a schoolmate from Wisconsin. All was well. The girls enjoyed the trip with their mother's solider friend, "Gid."

Clara and Pierson knew that this friend was Gideon. They were not pleased.

Seattle Times May 31,1908

FAMILY REUNITED BY VISIT OF FLEET

Chief Machinist Ellis of the *Kansas* Finds in Seattle Wife and Children He Had Not Seen for Eight Years

CALLS AT GREEN LAKE HOME WITHOUT NOTICE

Little Daughter Wonders Who the Visitor Is, and Mother Is Almost Speechless When She Recognizes Him.

Illustration 56. The text of the newspaper article printed on p. 12 of the *Seattle Times* on May 31, 1908, courtesy of Genealogybank.com, the Seattle Times archives.[67]

Seattle Times May 31, 1908

The coming of the Atlantic battle-ship fleet to Seattle was the means of reuniting a family at Green Lake that had been separated for eight years. Chief Machinist Gideon J. Ellis, of the battleship Kansas, had been here only two days when he discovered the woman from whom he had separated in the Black Hills of North Dakota so many years before and his two children, are living in this city.

When he reached the house of Mrs. Ellis, his 8-year old daughter, who was only two weeks old when the family parted in North Dakota, came to the door.

"There's a big soldier man here" she said to her mother, as she ran back to tell her. Mrs. Ellis went to the door.

"I was so surprised I was speechless" said Mrs. Ellis yesterday afternoon in describing her feelings. "The blood seemed to freeze in my veins. I was not entirely sure whether he was making a friendly visit or coming to kidnap the children.

There was a happy reunion, and after it was over, Ellis took mother and children through the labyrinth of the machinery on the Kansas. He was an electrical engineer when he lived in North Dakota. Interference of relatives, it is said caused the couple to separate, and Mrs. Ellis, with her children went to her parents' home in Wisconsin. A few months later she came to Seattle, where she has lived since. Working as a nurse to earn a living for herself and little ones.

Up to four years ago neither husband nor wife would admit a willingness to patch up their differences, when one of the little girls wanted to write to Santa Claus, Mrs. Ellis gave her the address of Mr. Ellis' parents in Michigan and the little girl wrote there. Not long after. A letter containing $5 for the little girl came from her father, but the letter was careful not to disclose the whereabouts to Mrs. Ellis. Sending the money first to his parents.

It is said that as soon as his term of enlistment expires Ellis will come to Seattle and rejoin his family.

Several days later, Alice read of her encounter with Gideon in the Sunday edition of the *Seattle Times*.[67] She was speechless. How dare Gideon break their agreement? The truth had been revealed. Alice was not a widow as she had told everyone that she was. After Alice and the girls had left the ship and returned home to Green Lake, Gideon had gone to a Seattle saloon for a few drinks. Alice suspected that he had coerced a reporter to print his version of the story. Alice was upset that he'd recounted personal conversations, which some were inaccurate. In addition, the article contained several lies or errors: the Black Hills are in South Dakota, Alice gave birth to Marie in Milwaukee, and Gideon had no intention of rejoining his family. Alice was livid to see this story, her story published for public viewing. She was adamant that the girls would not see or hear about this printed story.

Alice decided to take preemptive action. She asked Clara to spread the news to the church and community of Green Lake that this story was flawed and would hurt the children. The community responded. In home throughout Green Lake, page twelve of the Sunday paper was either missing or it quickly had made it to the burn pile.

Being a "grass widow" or divorcee was not an option for Alice. Alice would not amend her story. She maintained that she was a widow socially and in US censuses of 1910 and 1920.[5]

Unknown to Alice at the time, Gideon had remarried in 1900. His new wife, Annie, lived in Virginia.

Life is untrustworthy.

Illustration 57. Mount Rainier provides a dramatic backdrop for the world's fair in 1909. Permission granted from the University of Washington, Special Collections, Nowellx1040a.

MR. J.E. CHILBERG, PRESIDENT ALASKA-YUKON-
PACIFIC EXPOSITION, SEATTLE, WASH. I
CONGRATULATE YOU AND YOUR ASSOCIATION FOR
THE AUSPICIOUS OPENING OF THE ALASKA-YUKON-
PACIFIC EXPOSITION AND I CONGRATULATE THE
PEOPLE OF THE GREAT NORTHWEST ON THE COURAGE
AND ENTERPRISE THEY HAVE SHOWN IN BRINGING IT
FORTH
--WILLIAM H. TAFT
JUNE 1, 1909, 12:00 NOON PACIFIC TIME
WHITE HOUSE TELEGRAM[7]

9

1909~Going to the Fair

Alaska-Yukon-Pacific Exposition

Throughout the world, there are brave people who dare to travel the globe to explore and to discover faraway lands and cultures. A world's fair brings the world home. In 1909, the world was coming to Seattle. Nearly, 3.7 million people came to the fair between opening day, June 1, and closing day, October 16.[6, 7]

Alice's family was excited to take part in this historic event just two miles from their Green Lake home. Like many

Seattleites, they had spent several years doing their part to contribute to the fair.[7]

In January 1909, Myrtle and Marie came home from school and informed Alice that they were each required to write five letters to distant friends or family and invite them to come to Seattle and enjoy the fair. This was called "Home Letter Day."[7] On February 7, 1909, the entire family crafted letters, sending them to New York, Kansas, and Wisconsin. None of those invited attended, but they were invited nevertheless. March 9 was another letter-writing day in school. The girls wrote letters to children from other schools within the state.[7]

Alice knew that the fair would be a once-in-a-lifetime experience for her daughters, her parents, and herself. Seattle was diligently cleaning up the waterfront before the world came to town, and many brothels had been shut down. Alice's birthing business had decreased slightly. Additionally, the Washington State Nurses Association had been established in 1908 and had drafted the Nurse Practice Act, which was passed by the legislature in 1909. One candidate passed the exam in Seattle, George Smith.[68] It would be several years before Washington State would reinforce this law and soon Alice could no longer comfortably or legally advertise as a nurse, since she had not graduated nursing school and did not hold a diploma.

Property of Museum of History & Industry, Seattle

Illustration 58. A postcard advertising the world's fair. Reprinted per permission from the MOHAI.

Pierson, who was working for the city of Seattle as a street cleaner, was called on to contribute his expertise with mortar and stone in the building of the fair's exhibits. He spent countless hours of his own time, like other city workers, preparing for the exhibit before funding could be secured.[7] For two years prior to the fair's opening, he spent every working day at the site. He was honored to be part of an exhilarating event that his whole family could enjoy.

Illustration 59. A dirigible balloon hovers over the fairgrounds in 1909.
Permission granted from the University of Washington, Special
Collections, UW23078.

Samuel was three years old, Marie was nine, and Myrtle
was exactly eleven years old on June 1, 1909, opening day of
the exposition.[7] What a way to celebrate a birthday! The
whole family took the Wallingford streetcar to the fair. Clara
had spent the winter sewing clothes for everyone. They
stepped out dressed for the occasion. Pierson was able to
secure tickets for the family at a cost of fifty cents each for
three adults and twenty-five cents for each schoolchild.
Samuel was free.[7] They had ice cold lemonade for five cents.[7]

Illustration 60. Children's Day at the world's fair, June 5, 1909. Permission granted from the University of Washington, Special Collections, Nowellx2980.

June 5 was Children's Day at the fair, and the family returned.[7] They took every opportunity they could to attend. The things to do and sights to see were overwhelming. On one visit, a dirigible balloon flew over the fairgrounds. "Look in the sky!" Pierson told the girls. "It is an airship!" [7] The crowd roared with amazement.

Illustration 61. Igorrote dancers perform at the world's fair in 1909. Permission granted from the University of Washington, Special Collections, Frank Nowellx1557.

They went down to watch the Igorrote men, seminude tribesman from the Philippines, dancing on a platform on the Pay Streak, the fair's midway and sideshow area. Myrtle and Marie liked watching their mama and grandma's reaction to the dancing men even more than watching the men themselves! Clara and Alice were appalled. Pierson got up and started dancing like the Igorrote dancers. Clara gave him a stern look, and he stopped. The whole family laughed, except for Clara, of course. Later that summer, on September 15, an Igorrote baby was born on fairgrounds. The parents named the baby "President Taft." [7]

Life is amusing.

Illustration 62. The baby incubator exhibit at the world's fair. Permission granted from the University of Washington, Special Collections, Nowellx1628.

The baby incubator exhibit at the fair was a family favorite.[7, 69] Alice and the girls were both distressed and amazed to see the premature babies brought by the nurses in those metal boxes. Myrtle told Samuel, "Look, Sammy, you were even smaller than those babies." The family enjoyed the lectures given by the nurses who cared for the babies. The girls found out that a baby boy, "Ernest," was going to be raffled off by the Children's Home, an orphanage.[70] They pleaded with their mamma and grandma to buy raffle tickets to win a new brother. They were unsuccessful.

Illustration 63. Schoolchildren tour the world's fair in1909. Permission granted from the University of Washington, Special Collections, Nowellx2981.

On several occasions, Myrtle and Marie attended the fair free of charge with their school and teachers. They itched to return home and tell their grandpa about the Battle of Gettysburg Pavilion, where actors reenacted the battle, as Pierson was a veteran of the Civil War. Some of their favorite sites were the Asian exhibits, the Eskimo village, and the deep-sea divers display.[7] To their delight, Myrtle and Marie each earned a diploma for attending five educational sessions.

Illustration 64. The War Exhibit at the world's fair. Permission granted from the University of Washington, Special Collections, Nowellx2344.

Pierson went back to visit the war exhibit by himself.[7] It was a very meaningful occasion for him, as he had served in the Civil War from 1861-1863.[5] He was honored to see soldiers being memorialized. His heart was full of sorrow as he thought of the comrades whom he had left behind on the battlefield. Quiet tears came to his eyes.

Life is not to be forgotten.

Alice only went to the fair without her family on one day, and that was Woman's Suffrage Day, July 7,1909. She attended with friends from her Methodist congregation to listen to speakers call for women's right to vote. She brought back a balloon for Samuel that was imprinted with "Votes for Women." [7, 71]

Doc Brown told Alice that on July 21, the American Medical Association had a special day planned for all of Seattle physicians and their families. He took some time off from his busy practice. The AMA's focus on this family day was fighting the devastating disease of tuberculosis. [7] Doc Brown told Alice that his wife and children greatly enjoyed attending the fair with him. He realized that he needed to spend more time with them. They all went back to the fair again.

Illustration 65. People lined up for a ride on the "giggler" at the world's fair in this photo by Frank Nowell. Permission granted from the University of Washington, Special Collections, Nowellx1489.

Pierson decided to take Myrtle and Marie to Alki Ike's Wild West Show. He did not tell Alice or Clara, as he feared they might object to his plans. Instead, he told the ladies that he was taking the girls to the fair to ride the gigler (sic). Which he did. He just added the Alaskan-style Wild West show afterward.[7]

Life is fun.

Illustration 66. Performers in the Wild West Show at the world's fair pose for photographer Frank Nowell. Permission granted from the University of Washington, Special Collections, Nowellx2188.

The Wild West show, complete with lasso-swinging cowboys, Indians, and horses, was Pierson's favorite. Myrtle and Marie enjoyed watching their grandpa enjoy the show. He was yahoooing the whole time. He was having the time of his life. The cowboys fired their guns and twirled their lassos as they rode their ponies.[7] Pierson told the girls that all of this excitement was giving him the "backdoor trots." The girls were perplexed. Grandpa was so silly.

August 30 was Norway Day at the fair. Clara, Alice, and the girls went to the fair in the morning. Clara was proud of her Norwegian ancestry and kept written records. Pierson and Samuel arrived at noon, and together the entire family watched a majestic Viking ship arrive at Laurelhurst Bay.

Illustration 67. Norway Day at the 1909 world's fair. Permission granted from the University of Washington, Special Collections, UW14852.

Lincoln High School and Green Lake School took children to the fair on Saturday, September 11. It was King County Children's Day.[7] All of the children were admitted free of charge. They watched a vaudeville circus with clowns and jugglers. There was another Children's Day on Oct 9, and the girls returned for that day as well.[7]

As the last day of the fair approached, the whole family attended again on Oct. 2. They were excited to see the baby contest. Prizes were awarded for Prettiest Baby, Liveliest Baby, Best Red Hair, Fattest Baby, and the baby with the Best Taft Smile.[7] The girls wished that Samuel was younger. They knew he would have won a prize! There was plenty of crying on that day. In fact, all of the crying got Samuel crying.

This fair was Seattle's first world's fair and the first world's fair to make a profit.[7] Seattle sold the fair as the "Gateway to Alaska" as well as to the Yukon and Asia. As the fair ended, splendor dwindled. It was a fair not to be forgotten.

Illustration 68. Women's suffrage proponents post handbills in Seattle in 1910. Permission granted from the University of Washington, Special Collections, Curtis19943.

"Suffrage is a pivotal right."
~Susan B. Anthony

10

1910~Voting Rights

Suffrage for Washingtonian Women

Alice wanted a voice. She had been a longtime proponent of voting rights for women in Washington State. She frequently attended meetings throughout the city. In December, she was shocked to read in the paper that some of the same women who were speaking out for women's suffrage had failed to register to vote in school elections.[72] Alice was concerned that this could undermine the suffrage movement. She registered and was pleased to see her name printed in the *Sunday Seattle Times* with the names of 467 other women who had registered to vote in school elections.[72]

Carrie Middleton,
Alice A. Ellis,
Bessie Law,
Elizabeth A. S

Seattle Times   Dec 8 1908

—

POLITICAL RIGHTS WOMEN FAIL TO REGISTER

Leaders Who Have Advocated Most Strenuously Right of Sex to Vote Take No Interest in School Elections

468 OUT OF 43,000 QUALIFY THEMSELVES

Mrs. Fanny Leake Cuxxxngs, Mrs. Edward C. Fixx, Mrs. Bessie R. Sxxxxxx and Mrs. H.M. Hixx Delinquents

Illustration 69. The names of all 468 women who registered to vote, including Alice, were printed in a newspaper article on December 8, 1980. (Text acquired from Genealogybank.com, *Seattle Times*).

Alice was conflicted. She strongly supported women's right to vote but she knew it would affect her business. She knew that when women started to vote, there would be a call for morality, which would mean stamping out prostitution. That would drastically change her practice. In spite of this, Alice wanted her daughters to live in an honorable society where they could have a voice and be heard. She felt strongly about that. Further, she was tired of watching babies being discarded and worrying about their futures.

The region had a long history, extending over several decades, of attempts to extend the right to vote to women.

In 1854, Seattle pioneer Arthur Denny proposed a bill that would allow white women over the age of eighteen to vote .[72-74] It lost by one vote. Many people suspected that dissenters had been influenced by several lawmakers who were married to Indian women whom this law would not include.[72-74]

In 1883, a Women's suffrage bill was reintroduced and passed. On November 22, 1883, Washington Governor Gordon Newel signed the act, and it became law. Even though women only accounted for 38 percent of the electorate, women turned out at the polls in larger numbers than men did. Soon, the cry for law and order was heard in the booming West. Laws that would shut down brothels and saloons were proposed. But these laws would hinder many of the businesses that used brothels and saloons as a lure to get men to move out to the West.[72-74]

In 1889, a powerful business lobby suggested that women's suffrage could hamper the decision in Washington, DC, to grant statehood to the territory of Washington. The lobby succeeded in repealing the woman suffrage ammendment.[72-74] Again, women could not vote. Subsequently, the territory of Washington was granted statehood.

Finally, twenty-one years later on November 8, 1910, the right to vote was returned to women. Washington was the first state to grant women the right to vote in the twentieth century, an action that may have served as an impetus to other states, as well as the federal government, to finally sanction women's suffrage. Soon after, several states enacted similar laws. They included California in 1911 and Oregon, Arizona, and Kansas in 1912. The momentum continued. The nineteenth amendment to the US constitution was ratified and became law on August 26, 1920.[72-74]

Alice and many other Washingtonian women and men were pleased.

Illustration 70. Streetcar Seattle Ballard in 1918. (Courtesy of Seattle Municipal Archives, 12506.)

"The essential thing is to love the children and understand them."
~Mother Ryther

11

1912~Taking Him Back

Good Bye & Farewell

Samuel was six years old and had become a major part of the Ellis home in Green Lake. Though he had been born quite prematurely, his growth was not hampered. Myrtle, fourteen, and Marie, twelve, took tender care of him and were loving sisters. They played with him, took him swimming, went on walks, and even played army games with their dear Samuel. Nevertheless, Samuel needed a mother. Alice was extremely busy running their home and providing maternity care. Clara was Samuel's mother. She was there to love and discipline him.

School had started, and this year all three children were attending the Green Lake Grammar School. It was exciting for Myrtle and Marie to bring their little brother to school.[5] They kept a close watch on him.

Property of Museum of History & Industry, Seattle

Illustration 71. Children fishing off the boardwalk of Green Lake in 1909. Reprinted per permission from the MOHAI.

One Monday morning after the children left for school, Maggie appeared on Alice's doorstep. Maggie was the Alaskan woman who had prematurely given birth to Samuel. Alice welcomed her in for some coffee and to listen to her story.[5] Soon after Samuel's birth, Maggie had left prostitution for a respectful life in Juneau. She met a banker, and initially lived as his "left-handed wife." They eventually married, and

Maggie was becoming a woman of society. She was barren.

Maggie pleaded with Alice to let her reclaim her son. She had told her husband, who was in Juneau, that Samuel was the son of a cousin, and she would be bringing him back.

Alice knew that she had no right to keep Samuel.[5]

Alice walked down to the school and spoke with the principal. The principal released Samuel to go home with Alice. Alice left word for the girls not to look for Samuel, saying that she had already taken him home.

Alice carefully explained to Samuel that his aunt had returned to pick him up and that he would be moving to an exciting place called Alaska. He cried. She took him to his room to gather his belongings. They walked out to the parlor. Maggie grabbed him by his little arm and took him out to the carriage, where a driver was waiting. Once again, Maggie was gone just as quickly as she had arrived.

Alice did not have the heart to take him next door to say good-bye to Clara. Alice was broken as she walked back to the house. She glanced at her mama's house and noticed Clara peeking through the curtains.

How would Alice explain to the girls and Clara what had happened? What could she say? The girls and Clara didn't speak to Alice for weeks.

Life is sad.

~*~

Seattle was seeing an increase in unwanted children left homeless by illness, neglect, or the death of parents. In the Northwest, parents often did not have the support of extended families. In 1885, Ollie Ryther promised a dying neighbor that she would take care of her four children. After that, Ollie Ryther vowed never to turn an orphan away. She soon became known as Mother Ryther.[75, 76]

Mother Ryther and Alice lived in the Green Lake – Wallingford areas north of Seattle and were colleagues.[5] They both had experience of working with prostitutes in Seattle and belonged to the same denomination (Methodist). So perhaps, many women who delivered in Alice's home sought a home for their child at Mother Rythers' City Mission Foundling Home for unwed mothers and their babies. [75, 76]

In the later years, circa 1915, Mother Ryther did ask Alice to take in a foundling. Alice did offer them a temporary home.[5, 75] Since Alice was the sole supporter of her home she did receive payments for the care that she gave.

Illustration 72. Mother Ryther and a child. (Courtesy of Ryther.org.

Illustration 73. A woman and a baby in the 1900s. (Library of Congress.)

By the 1920s, the nursing and midwifery professions were becoming more regulated and the rules were being reinforced. Alice could no longer advertise her services as nursing care. The times were changing in other ways, too. More women were choosing to give birth in hospitals, which had begun to offer "twilight sleep" for pain relief, replacing chloroform and ether. Alice's birthing home would soon become a baby home— at least publically.

Illustration 74. Clara E. Wood in 1862 in Bath, New York.[5]

"A Mother is the truest friend we have. When trials heavy and sudden fall upon us; when adversity takes the place of prosperity; when friends desert us; when trouble thickens around us, still will she cling to us, and endeavor by her kind precepts and counsels to dissipate the clouds of darkness, and cause peace to return to our hearts."

~Washington Irving

12

1914~Losing Mama:

Clara E. Wood 1834-1914

Clara was eighty years old when she died. She died in her own Green Lake home, surrounded by the people who knew and loved her best: Pierson, Alice, Myrtle, Marie, and her son, Eddie. She would join her oldest daughter, Beulah, who had died in Seattle in 1901, in the heavens above. The only person missing was her dear Samuel.

Clara was born in New York in 1834 to James and Mary French. Her ancestors had been in the colonies that would become the United States since the mid-1600s. She was particularly proud of her Norwegian and Scandinavian heritage. Her ancestors included New York heir Anneke Jans Bogardus, who had a large amount of land on Manhattan Island in New York City. She was buried at Trinity Church near Wall Street on Manhattan Island, which is still standing. Anneke was born 1605 in Flekkeroy, Norway, and was married in 1624 to Jans Roeloffsen, born 1600 in Masterlant, Sweden.[5]

Green Lake and Seattle, in general, reminded Clara of the meaningful customs and traditions of her ancestor. She kept her culture alive by baking or cooking traditional Swedish dishes and sung Swedish lullabies to Samuel and the girls at night. Clara also was a fan of Alice's blackberry pie.

~*~

Illustration 75. Mary French, Clara's mother; Clara E. French Wood; and Callie French, Clara's sister. Photographed in the dining room of the French home in Bath, Steuben County, New York, in 1862.[5]

In New York, Clara met and married Pierson, and they loaded up a wagon and traveled west to Madison, Wisconsin, to be close to Pierson's family. They soon moved to Milwaukee, it was there that they raised their three children and soon the established a beautiful home in the Milwaukee suburb of Wauwatosa.[5]

Like Alice, Clara was known for her natural capacity to care for others. She was always creating new remedies for pain and illness.[5] For pioneer women, providing good health care for the family was an important contribution.

Clara had her own philosophy of helping women give birth. She was in charge, and they knew it. Her approach was pragmatic. She gave the mothers meaningful tasks, such as kneading dough and churning butter, to distract them from the pain of contractions.[5] She was called upon by others in her community to help with birthing and other frontier healthcare. Most women found it helpful. Her own daughter, Alice, was not one of these women.

Initially, Alice vowed never to have her women do "those" tasks during childbirth. However, Alice discovered that mother was right: women in labor often coped better if they were given a manual task on which to focus.
Life is peculiar.

Clara was particularly saddened when Samuel's birth mother took him to Alaska. Helping Myrtle and Marie take care of the boy had brought her joy. She had grown to love the little boy. Clara's health declined after Samuel left with his mother. In her last months, she was very weak and rarely left home. Clara passed away in her loving husband's arms at the age of seventy-nine.[5]

Marie, Alice and Myrtle Ellis

Illustration 76. It is believed that Alice, forty-six, took her girls to Seattle to have this professional photograph made shortly after the death of her mother in abt 1914. Marie age 14 on the left, Alice, Myrtle age 16 on the right.[5]

Illustration 77. Seattle residents wear masks as a precaution against illness during the Great Pandemic of 1918. (National Archives.)

"Only a life lived for others is a life worthwhile."
~Albert Einstein

13

1918~Tending to the Flu:

The Great Pandemic

As death claims the lives of those we love, we cling a little tighter to those who remain. The Great Flu was coming, and Seattleites were scared. Nevertheless, the city was ready. It had time on its side. The flu was traveling from the eastern side of the country. The local health authorities distributed masks and made wearing them mandatory. It also distributed vaccines. Later, looking back, epidemiologists claimed that only the vaccines were helpful.[77-80] It was reported that 10,000 ship workers received flu vaccines, and not one reported the flu.[77-80] On the other hand, using masks to protect oneself against the extremely small flu virus can be compared to using chicken wire to keep dust out of a cage.

This global pandemic took at least 21 million to their graves, and 700,000 of those deaths occurred in the United States. On October 3, 1918, at the University of Washington Naval Training Station in Seattle, 700 cases of flu and one death were reported. Over the next six months, more than 1,600 people in Seattle would die in the deadly pandemic.[77-80]

The city of Seattle issued ordinances banning spitting, dancing, and gathering—including gathering at Sunday services. Many of the ministers were understandably upset. Mayor Ole Hanson responded, "Religion that won't keep for two weeks is not worth having." [77]

On November 11, 1918, armistice was announced between the allies and Germany. Thousands of people rallied in the streets to celebrate, and there were no masks in sight. The flu resurged.[77-80]

~*~

Alice's family, like many families in Seattle, was apprehensive. Alice had not been delivering very many babies in her home. However, some women were afraid to go to the hospital for fear they would be exposed to the flu. So Alice opened her door to a few women to bear their children. By December, the flu was again rapidly spreading throughout the city. [77-80]

Alice noticed that the Danklefsen family, her neighbors across the street, was not leaving their home.[81] They had recently immigrated from Sweden and did not know the neighbors very well. The family had chickens in the backyard. Marie, now eighteen, had told Alice that on the way back from her work as a telephone operator, she had noticed that the chickens were fighting. It appeared that they were not being fed.[81] So Alice decided that when her father got home, they would see what was going on.

Alice wrapped Pierson up with sheets and he went to the Danklefsen's home. He knocked. No one answered. He opened the door. The family had all gathered in the chilly living room, trying to warm one another with wool blankets The stove was not on. They could barely speak. Pierson reassured them that he would be back. He went home and told Alice what had happened. Alice immediately took action. She created a salty broth for Pierson to give to the family. Alice sent Marie over with feed and water for the chickens. They continued this routine on a daily basis for two weeks.[81]

Pierson went to the Danklefsen home every morning and every evening, before and after work, and spoon-fed each member of the family for two weeks. They all lived.[81]

Many years later, Mr. Danklefsen told Pierson that the whole family had had the flu, and they were afraid to leave their home. They were afraid that people would blame them for the deadly outbreak. So, day-by-day, they became more ill. They had recovered from the flu, but were starving and too weak to cry for help. Every Christmas from then on, Mrs. Danklefsen brought over Swedish *knack* and *peparkakor* for Pierson and the Ellises to eat.

Several months later, a little boy came knocking at Alice's door and said, "Please, Alice, hurry! My grandpa can't breathe—he has the flu. My momma said you can save him." So Alice hurried over, taking with her some turpentine to cut the phlegm. She had the man gargle with it; enabling him to breathe.[5] She saved his life.[5]

Alice saved lives. She wasn't as busy with birthing anymore, but she was busy she continued to offer care and work with Seattle doctors. The immigrant families were particularly welcoming of her homemade remedies.

Life is sacred.

Illustration 78. Washington state police line the streets during the 1918 flu. (National Archives.)

Illustration 79. Pierson Wood in Seattle in abt 1910, when he was about seventy-four years old.[5]

"Without hard work, nothing grows but weeds."
~Gordon B. Hinckley

14

1922~Remembering Father

Pierson E. Wood 1836-1922

Pierson Edgar Wood was the first one of the family to venture out west to Seattle in 1900. Years earlier, he had chosen wisely when he'd built a home in the up-and-coming town of Wauwatosa, Wisconsin. Proceeds of the sale of that home enabled him to build two homes—his and Alice's—in the Seattle suburb of Green Lake, Washington.

Pierson was born in a log cabin in Bath, New York, in June 1836 to Algernon Sydney Wood (approximately1814-1871) and Sarah Ann Brant (approximately 1817-1858). He was the oldest of four. Brothers S.A. Wood, Albert, and Benjamin followed. The young family left their log cabin in Steuben County, New York, to pursue a new life in the frontier town of Madison, Wisconsin, around 1840. It was there that the youngest two sons were born. [5]

Illustration 80. This 1840s' photo shows the log cabin where Benjamin Wood was born in the frontier land of Madison Wisconsin.[5]

Algernon S. Wood
1859

Illustration 81. Pierson's father, Algeron S. Wood.[5]

Pierson's father, Algernon, was born in New Jersey. When he resettled his family in Madison, Wisconsin, he worked as a journeyman stonecutter, a trade he passed on to Pierson. In 1850, Governor Dewey of Wisconsin appointed Algernon to procure, dress, and inscribe a slab of white marble, which would be sent to Washington, DC, to be used in the Washington Monument.[5] It was an honor.

Illustration 82. The stone that Algernon Wood created for the Washington Monument. Wisconsin was admitted to the union in 1848. This stone represented Wisconsin's commitment to its country.[5]

Pierson was a good-natured and well-liked man. He loved being out West; he was a cowboy at heart. No one adored him more than Myrtle and Marie did.[5] If they needed a laugh, they went next door to see their grandpa.

On the Fourth of July in 1909, during the world's fair, Pierson had a surprise for the girls. He had located some firecrackers and wanted to show the girls how brave he was. Pierson misjudged the timing and *BAM,* the firecracker exploded in his hand! [82]

The girls grabbed their grandpa and took him to the house, where Alice and Clara were cooking. Alice looked at Pierson in astonishment. "Father, you really did it this time!"

Luckily, she determined that his wounds were minor. "You are burned and bruised, but not seriously injured," she said.

"You will live." They all had a laugh, even Pierson.[82]

Seattle Times   July 4th 1909

GRANDFATHER GETS HIS HAND HURT

73-Year-Old Man Allows Firecracker to Explode in his Hand While Celebrating With Children

---

GREEN LAKE, Saturday July 4- Helping his grandchildren to celebrate today, P. Wood 73 years old who resides at XXXX   North XXXXXX Street met with an accident. Wood was having as much fun as the children until he held a big firecracker in his hand too long after lightening it. There was an explosion and Wood thought his hand had been blown to fragments. When he went into the home of his daughter Mrs. Alice Ellis, next door, to receive attention, he found, however, that his hand, although somewhat bruised and powder burned, was not seriously injured.

Illustration 83. The newspaper article and the text above was retrieved from Genealogybank.com, the *Seattle Times* archives.

Pierson spent the first sixty years of life as a stonecutter, like his father, Algernon. In 1900, at sixty-four years of age, he resettled his family in Seattle, securing a job with the city as a street cleaner. He earned a salary of $2.25 a day.[28] By 1918, his city salary had doubled to $4.50 a day.[28] Family and public records suggest he worked for the city until he died at eighty-six in 1922.[5]

Illustration 84. This 1920 photo shows a Seattle city street cleaner in operation. It is probably like the one that Pierson drove. (Courtesy of the Seattle Municipal Archives, Item 1729.)

Pierson loved grooming his horses and taking care of his town. He also continued to work with stone. In 1910 when construction of the Methodist church began in Green Lake, Pierson contributed his skills as a stonecutter.

Illustration 85. Pierson is most likely in this 1918 photo of the Methodist church in Green Lake. Pierson, a journeyman stonecutter, volunteered his time and expertise in creating this magnificent building. (Photo dated November, 26, 1918, used courtesy of United Methodist Church, Green Lake, Washington.)

Illustration 84. Pierson, left, with his brothers, Benjamin, center, and Albert.[5]

After Clara died in 1914, Pierson felt compelled to take a train to the Midwest to visit his brothers, Albert and Benjamin, who were both living in Kansas at the time. It was a grand reunion and the three men, all in their seventies, went to be photographed as a celebration—good lives well lived.[5]

~*~

Pierson had not taken his wife's death in 1914 well. He continued to spend most of his day working for the city of Seattle, but returned to Alice's home after work each evening for a home-cooked meal and blackberry pie. Eventually, Alice and Pierson decided to sell Pierson's home, and he moved in with his daughter. It is believed that these funds helped Alice with her finances well into the end of her own life.

Pierson watched, as his beautiful granddaughters became fine young women. From 1912 to 1918, Myrtle and Marie attended Lincoln High School in Seattle.[5, 25] Myrtle was a violinist in the school orchestra.[25] Myrtle and Marie were quite striking and drew attention from local young gents. Marie wrote to a few gentleman callers, who were serving in the military during World War I.[5]

One evening Marie came home late and was kissing her gentleman friend good-bye on the porch. Alice started flickering the porch light on-and-off. A subtle sign that grandpa and her were watching and time to stop. [5]

Myrtle and Marie were very helpful with Alice and her business and for the care of their dear grandpa. However, like most teenagers they desired to create their own path as they matured and discovered the world.

Property of Museum of History & Industry, Seattle

Illustration 86. Myrtle and Marie attended Lincoln High School in Seattle. 1911. PEMCO Webster & Stevens Collection, Reprinted with permission granted from the MOHAI.

Pierson was amused watching how Alice disciplined her high-school daughters. One day Myrtle and Marie had left their clothes all over the second floor of their home. As the girls returned from school, they noticed a big pile of clothes on their front lawn. Their mother, Alice, had thrown their clothes out of the second story window.[5] The message was clear. They did not leave their clothes on the floor anymore.

In 1918, Myrtle married a young man named Ernie Smith. Smith was his American name. He had emigrated from Ukraine. [25] Alice called him an "a Bolshevik."

Myrtle quickly became pregnant. Of course, Myrtle knew the best place to have a baby was in her childhood home, and best person to assist her in delivery was her mother. Alice welcomed Myrtle back into the Green Lake home and assisted in the birth of her first grandchild—and Pierson's great-grandchild—on March 17, 1919. Myrtle named the baby Iris. Both Alice and Myrtle loved flowers. Alice belonged to a Flower society in Seattle.[5]

During this time Marie, who was nineteen, graduated from high school and went to work as a telephone operator.[5]

By the 1920s, Pierson was the only person whom Alice cared for in her home. Pierson died in Alice's home on December 15, 1922, he was and is still loved.

In the same place where Alice helped bringing babies into the world, she was now assisting those closest to her in death.

Seattle Times December 15th 1922, p. 2
Aged City Employee Dies
Funeral Services for Pierson A. Wood 86 years old, who died yesterday at the home of his daughter Mrs. Alice A. Ellis, xxxx N. xx[nd] St. Services were held this afternoon at 2 o'clock at the Butterworth Mortuary, followed by cremation. Mr. Wood was born in New York State and came to Seattle twenty-two years ago. He had been a member of the city Street Department eighteen years. Mrs. Ellis is the only relative surviving.

Illustration 87. Pierson Wood's obituary appeared on p. 2 of the *Seattle Times* on December 16, 1922. It was not quite accurate, since his brothers, his granddaughters, and two great-grandchildren also survived him. (Text acquired from Genealogybank.com, *Seattle Times*.)

Property of Museum of History & Industry, Seattle

Illustration 88. A *Seattle Times* photo of a "Hooverville" in 1930 in Seattle. Reprinted per permission from the MOHAI.

"Courage is resistance to fear, mastery of fear, not absence of fear."
~Mark Twain

15

1929~Surviving

Seattle's Great Depression

The Great Depression fell upon the country after the fall of the stock market in 1929 and soon penetrated nearly every home in America. Seattle was hit extremely hard as the Depression intensified in the 1930s. Nearly one out of four workers was unemployed.[83-84] The logging industry was hit particularly hard, with more than 50 percent unemployment. Many people who still had jobs saw a decrease in their salaries.[83-84]

At that time, there was no government-sponsored unemployment insurance, and soon people were losing their homes. Encampments of tents and poorly constructed shacks appeared throughout Seattle. In 1931, Seattle's "Hooverville" was located in the mud flats by Elliot Bay. Hoovervilles, which arose in many cities across the United States, were named after the president, whom many blamed for the Depression. Seattle's Hooverville remained until 1941, when the city tore it down.[83-84]

The term "Skid Road" originated in Seattle. Loggers skidded logs down the steep Seattle hills to sawmills located on the waterfront. Eventually, the term evolved to Skid Row, which often referred to the seedy side of town, typically inhabited by drunks and transients. Pioneer Square at one time claimed this title.[83, 84]

Desperation led to crime. Seattle saw an increase in murders, robberies, and suicides. The crime rate hit an all-time high in 1932.[83, 84]

~*~

Alice was a strong and capable woman. She survived the Depression. She had planned well and was able to withstand economic hardships. Social Security benefits were not enacted until 1935, she had received none.

Shortly after Pierson's passing in 1923, Marie had made an announcement. "I am moving to Los Angeles, California!"[5]

Alice had been speechless. How could Marie move so far away?

Marie had explained that rent was cheap there, and there were plenty of jobs in the Golden State.[5] In 1923, Marie moved down to Los Angeles with a lady friend and in a very short time met a man at a community dance, William Harrison McMillen. Harry was an Irishman from the silver-mining town of Durango, Colorado.[5]

The relationship infuriated Alice, who was of Dutch, English, and Scandinavian descent. How could her daughter marry an Irishman—and worse yet, a Catholic?[5] First, Myrtle married a Russian - Ukrainian, and now Marie, an Irishman.[5] Could her daughters make any poorer choices for a spouse?

But Alice was a survivor, and her disappointment in their choices paled in the face of the struggles caused by the Great Depression.

The Depression forced Myrtle, Ernie, and their two children, Iris and Donald, who were still living in Green Lake to move back to the Green Lake home with Alice. There, they could pool their money and make ends meet during this time of financial mayhem.[5]

Life is uncertain.

One late summer afternoon in the mid-1920s, Alice's doorbell rang.

Her parents both had died, her daughters both had married and moved out. Alice was living alone in her Green Lake home. She answered the door, and there on her doorstep stood a large, handsome young man, perhaps twenty years of age.[5]

It was Samuel.

He had returned to see the home where he was born, raised, and loved. He was saddened to hear that Clara and Pierson had died. However, he was very happy to hear that Myrtle was married and had two children, and that Marie was married to a good man in Los Angeles. He had traveled down from Alaska and decided to stop by for a visit and indulge in his much loved and missed good cooking. They both had a delicious piece of Alice's blackberry pie. It was a joyous reunion for them both.[5]

Life is wonderful.

Epilogue

Alice Ada Wood Ellis

(April 14, 1868-July 3, 1936).

Alice died of stomach cancer in 1936. She had sold her Green Lake home and bought a home in Edmonds, Washington, where she lived until she became ill. She had moved in with Myrtle and her family so they could take care of her.[5, 23] Gideon sent money to Myrtle to pay for a marker for her grave. Her legacy of hard work and great love lives on. Alice Ada Wood Ellis, a midwife, nurse, and mother to all, was truly a Seattle pioneer.

Life is eternal.

Illustration 89. Alice Ada Wood Ellis was sixty-one in this photo, 1929.

Myrtle June Clarabelle Ellis Smith

(June 1, 1898-March 1, 1954)

In 1918, Myrtle married Ernie Smith, who was born in Lutsk, Ukraine. They had two children, Iris and Donald. Iris was born in Alice's home on March 17, 1919. Donald was also born in a home (one street over from Alice's in Green Lake) on August 25, 1921.

Myrtle worked as a secretary for a company on Western Avenue along "produce row" in Seattle. The owner, M. L. Davies, even put Myrtle in charge of one of his businesses. At one time, Myrtle and Ernie employed a housekeeper/nanny who took care of the children, cleaned house, and made dinner. At times, Alice took care of Iris and Donald while their parents worked. They both loved Grandma's cooking.[23] Marie called Myrtle a "career woman." She admired her sister.

Myrtle died of heart disease.

*Mother Myrtle,
daughter Iris and son Don*

Illustration 90. In this 1927 photo, Iris is eight, Myrtle is twenty-nine, and Donald is six.

Beulah Marie Ellis McMillen
(June 6, 1900-January 17, 1990)

Marie stayed in Los Angeles, and she did marry Harry despite her sister's warnings against the match. (Below, see excerpts from Myrtle's five-page letter to Marie, written in January 1923.)

To Alice's astonishment, for the first five years Marie did not have children. Alice told Marie, "After you have relations with your husband, stand on your head for at least five minutes." Marie followed her advice, and lo and behold, she gave birth to three boys over the next four years. The first two, Billy and Bobby, were "Irish twins" born only ten months apart.

Billy (William Harrison McMillen, Jr., born May 2, 1927) is the father of author Susan Fleming. Billy and Bobby (Robert, born in March 1928) were gifted runners. Bob did not make the Eagle Rock high school track team like his brother Bill. However, Bob did win a silver medal in the 1,500-meter race at the 1952 Olympic Games in Helsinki, Finland. He beat Roger Bannister in that race (first man to break the 4-minute mile.)

Marie died in 1990 with a few of her children at her bedside and was able to give an "Old Dutch" smile, minutes before she passed away to be with the Lord.

In the summer of 1929, Harry and Marie took the train to Seattle with their two young sons. Alice and Myrtle were thrilled to see her and meet the two little boys.[5]

Illustration 91. Marie, twenty-nine, visiting Green Lake, with her two boys, Robert Earl McMillen and William Harrison McMillen, Jr., on the bottom step. At top right is Myrtle's daughter, Iris. Her brother, Donald, stands below her. The other children are perhaps neighbors.

Jan. 17, 1923

My Dear Marie,

We just received your letter…We were both shocked and surprised…Now Marie, I am going to try to give you a little kindly advice…you are only 22 years old…Harry has been married before and thought the world… of this wife. Now Marie, can't you see that it would be awfully hard for him to find another wife to quite take the place…He is very likely to compare the things his second does and the way she keeps house with his first wife…apt to occasionally throw things like this at his second wife, such as "Molly didn't do this or did do that."…And now another thing Marie, you say he is a Catholic. Now Marie, you have been raised a strict Protestant. You should understand what marrying a Catholic means. First, you would be married by a priest, you who have never so much as been to a Catholic Church service. Secondly, your children would be reared Catholics—absolutely. Another thing, Marie, that you may not know, a Catholic believes you should NOT DO A THING to stop having children. You should not even do a thing to prevent getting pregnant, as every child is God sent, as it were. Now, you ought to know what that means, Marie, a child every year. In keep you from getting pregnant, much less use something himself such as Ernie is doing for me. You know Marie you have only known Harry for three months. Now Marie, I beg of you to please think of everything before you take the fatal plunge. First of all, do you truly love him or is it just a sort of fascination? Does he truly love you? HOW MUCH MONEY HAS HE IN THE BANK! Is he stingy, or will he loosen up his purse strings to you.   *Your loving sister, Myrtle*

Gideon J. Ellis

(May 31 1868-May 1940)

This book does not reflect Gideon Ellis's untold story. Gideon retired from the US Navy with the rank of lieutenant. He hired a private investigator to locate Alice and the girls in the 1930s. Alice, who was terminally ill at the time, was upset by this action, but she did give Marie's contact information to him. Sadly, unbeknownst to Alice and the girls, Gideon was dying, too. He offered to pay Marie and Myrtle's train fare if they would travel to Virginia to meet him and his current wife, Annie, whom he had married in 1904. They did not have any children.

Myrtle was unable to leave work, but Marie did take the train to Virginia. She later said that she "had a magnificent time" meeting their father and his wife for the first time." Several years later, Gideon and Annie died, leaving their estate, which included a home and an apartment building, to Myrtle and Marie. This act of genuine love and kindness was welcomed. We don't know you Gideon, but we love you.

About the Author

Susan Fleming trained as a diploma nurse at Los Angeles County School of Nursing. She earned her BSN at the WSU Intercollegiate College of Nursing in Spokane. She received a MN degree and perinatal clinical nurse specialist certification at the University of Washington School of Nursing in Seattle, and she returned to WSU CON in Spokane for her PhD.

Susan is fortunate to do what she loves, which is teaching nursing and conducting research on birthing. She listens to mothers' birthing stories as well as mothers' experiences with self-education using the Internet and mobile phones. Today, she is as an assistant professor at WSU CON in Spokane, where Dr. Roxanne Vandermause, Dr. Cindy Corbett and Dr. Billie Severtsen have influenced her love for writing and research. She serves on the boards of the March of Dimes in

Seattle and a national website exceptionalnurse. com. She lives in Washington with her husband, and they are the parents of seven amazing children.

Illustration 93. In 1986, Susan is with her dad Bill and Marie, her grandmother, sharing her own birth story of her first-born "Dana Rose."

Acknowledgments

To my beloved husband, Ed, and daughter, Dana, thank you for being my appointed editors. Ed's experience with birthing provided a valuable resource for this book. To my treasured great-grandmother, Alice Ada Wood Ellis; and her parents, Pierson and Clara Wood, I offer tribute and grew to love you more. To my beloved paternal grandmother, Marie Ellis McMillen, who shared stories of Alice's courageous life with me, I give thanks. I extend love to Marie and Harry's children: my dad, Bill (Dorothy); uncles, Bob (Joan) and Tom (Joan); and aunts, Mary (Paul) and Joanne (Fred); my mother, Dorothy; my brothers, Ed and John; my sister, Nancy Marie, who is a nurse; and my children, Dana, Harrison, Annika, Monika, Kristina, Sasha, and Bogdan, who allow me to mother.

I extend special thanks to Myrtle and Ernie's children, Iris Smith (Bud) Ramey and Donald Quinn Smith; and their children, my second cousins Carol, Allison, Dean, Barbara, Beth, Brian, and Tim. Many of them shared their revered stories and pictures. Thank you.

Thanks to all of my cousins on my father's side, Bonnie, Patrick, Cathy, Wayne, Marie also a nurse, Jeffrey, Daniel, Michael, Glenn, and Colleen; and nephews, nieces, and in-laws Mary, Debbie, Jessica future nurse, LinDe, and Madison. Knowing these people for many years has enlightened me to the courage and strength of our cherished family.

Appendix

Author's Notes

Chapter 1: Personal accounts written over the years indicate that the family moved to Seattle December 1900. Official records confirm this date. My research turned up the Great Northern Flyer.

Chapter 2: Milwaukee School of Engineering School of Nursing is the school Alice most likely attended. It had a two-year nursing program. I knew Alice had completed the first year of a two-year program Abigail and Nurse Campbell are fictitious.

Chapter 3: Elizabeth's birthing story is based on Marie's husband Harry's first wife, who died at 7 months pregnant in his arms.

Chapter 4: Alice did connect with many doctors to assist with births in her home. Dr. Brown is a pseudonym based on stories that have been passed. Sister Mary Agnes is fictitious. Some of the accounts are based on Alice's stories, while others are fictitious.

Chapter 5: Many professionals, such as doctors, moved to Seattle to help with the population explosion. William Wood, who donated land for the first school in Green Lake, was from San Francisco, so in this story, I selected Nob Hill as the birth place of Dr. Brown, who is fictitious. Jesse and Ella are fictitious characters based on an actual birth experience.

Chapter 6: Alice did take care of women who birthed in her home, many of whom were prostitutes from Alaska and the Yukon. Samuel's tale is based on a true story. The mother's names are either pseudonyms or the characters themselves are fictitious, and their stories are based on my own births and my forty years of experience with birthing.

Chapter 7: The bubonic plague story is believed to be true, based on family stories. Alice was respected and asked to confirm the plaque then sent to quarantine. Secrecy was demanded. Cannot confirm if the city or health department picked up Alice. Fecal implants are used today to fight off c-diff infections with a cure rate of 90 percent, according to the Mayo Clinic.

Chapter 8: The stories about the world fair are based on my family's interests. Alice and her family lived only two miles from the fairgrounds, and Marie told me in 1967 that they attended the fair many times.

Chapter 10: Samuel is pseudonym for a real baby who was born prematurely in Alice's home. He lived with the Ellises until he was six, and returned for a visit as a man. His birth mother was a prostitute from Alaska.

Chapter 12: Accounts of the flu are based on true stories from family members. Alice was involved with helping others during the flu outbreak. The Danklefsen tale based on a story that my father-in-law, Ralph Danklefsen, told about the way his family cared for neighbors during the flu pandemic in 1918.

Despite her mothers' and sister's warnings against marrying Harry, Marie was fortunate to have found a very good man. Together, they had five children (Billy, Bobby, Tommy, Joanne, and Mary).

Illustration 92. Alice's four grandsons, photographed in Los Angeles in abt 1944. From left, William Harrison McMillen, seventeen; Thomas McMillen, fourteen; Donald Quinn Smith, twenty; and Robert Earl McMillen, sixteen.

Illustration 93. Alice's two of her three beautiful granddaughters, Joanne Marie and Mary Kathleen. Marie's girls photographed in Los Angeles abt the 1960s. Aunt Mary and Susan talk frequently about Alice, Marie and Clara.

References

1. Doyle, Ted. *Great Northern Flyer.* Retrieved from http://www.gnflyer.com/Flyer3.html.

2. Muller, C. (1996). *James J. Hill. Rail Serve.com.* Retrieved from http://www.railserve.com/JJHill.html.

3. Great Northern History. Retrieved from http://www.gnrhs.org/gn_history.htm.

4. Great Northern Empire. Retrieved from http://www.greatnorthernempire.net/.

5. Marie Ellis McMillen's personal story told to Susan Fleming and Mary McMillen Montejano. Recollections of Carol Deming Solle, Barbara Imbrie, and Brian Ramey; and family records and pictures.

6. Berner, R. (1991). *Seattle 1900-1920: From Boomtown, Urban Turbulence to Restoration.* Seattle: Charles Press.

7. Stein, A., P. Becker, and HistoryLink staff. (2009). *Alaska-Yukon-Pacific Exposition Washington's First World's Fair: A Timeline History.* Seattle: HistoryLink/University of Washington Press.

8. Colbert, D. (1998). *"Butch Cassidy and the Sundance Kid Rob a Train, 1899."* Eyewitness to History, the American West. Retrieved from http://www.eyewitnesstohistory.com/cassidy.htm.

9. Butch Cassidy. Retrieved from http://www.utah.com/oldwest/butch_cassidy.htm.

10. *Anaconda Standard*, July 3, 1901. Text of Butch Cassidy

article is from Genealogybank.com.

11. Hughes, T. *"Last train Robbery of Butch Cassidy and the Sundance kid." Rare and early newspapers.* Retrieved from http://www.rarenewspapers.com/view/562002.

12. HistoryLink.org. Online encyclopedia of Washington State history. "George Webster Is Hanged for First-Degree Murder at Spokane County Courthouse on March 30, 1900." Essay 10258 by Daryl C. McClary. Retrieved from http://www.historylink.org/index.cfm.

13. HistoryLink.org. Online encyclopedia of Washington State history. "State of Washington Conducts Its Last Execution by Hanging on May 27, 1994." Essay 5555 by David Wilma. Retrieved from http://www.historylink.org/index.cfm.

14. Leifer, S. (2010). Histories. "The History of the Milwaukee School of Engineering School of Nursing." Retrieved from http://resources.msoe.edu/library/archive/digital/mss01/Hist/historyoftheschoolofnursingatmsoeindex.html

15. Starr,P. (1982). *The Social Transformation of American Medicine.* New York: Basic Books.

16. "The Making of Milwaukee." Retrieved from http://www.themakingofmilwaukee.com/index.cfm.

17. City of Deadwood. History. Retrieved from http://www.cityofdeadwood.com.

18. Blackburn, S. (2007). *Maternal, Fetal, and Neonatal Physiology.* A Clinical Perspective. (3rd ed.). St. Louis: Saunders.

19. London, M., Ladewig, P., Davidson, M., Ball, J., Bindler, R. & Cowen, K. (2014). *Maternal & Child Nursing Care.* 4th ed. Upper Saddle River, NJ: Pearson/Prentice Hall

20. Potter, P., & Perry, A. (2013). *Fundamentals of Nursing.* 8th ed. St. Louis Missouri: Elsevier

21. Lambskin condoms FAQ. Retrieved from http://www.lambskincondoms.org.

22. DeLee, J. B. (1904). *Obstetrics for Nurses* (1st ed.). Philadelphia: W.B. Saunders Company.

23. Wertz, R. and D. Wertz. (1989). *Lying-in A History of Childbirth in America.* New Haven: Yale University Press.

24. Rook, J. (1997). *Midwifery & Childbirth in America.* Philadelphia: Temple University Press.

25. Written accounts of Alice's granddaughter, Iris Smith Ramey, or grandson, Donald Quinn Smith.

26. HistoryLink.org. Online encyclopedia of Washington State history. "Transportation and Communication in Seattle 1900." Essay 1668 by James Warren. Retrieved from http://www.historylink.org/index.cfm.

27. Morgan, L. (1998). *Good Time Girls.* Fairbanks, Alaska: Epicenter Press.

28. HistoryLink.org. Online encyclopedia of Washington State history. "Wood, William D. (1858-1917)." Essay 1169 by Louis Fiset, Green Lake Park Alliance, May 30, 1999. Retrieved from http://www.historylink.org/index.cfm.

29. HistoryLink.org. Online encyclopedia of Washington State

history. "Green Lake School (Seattle)." By Louis Fiset, October 9,1999. Retrieved from http://www.historylink.org/index.cfm.

30. HistoryLink.org. Online encyclopedia of Washington State history. "Stone Cutters Form a Union During March 1889." By Greg Lange, May 9,1999.

31. Seattle Municipal Archives. P.F. Wood's Work Card.

32. Maranzani, B. (2013). "Eight Things You May Not Know about the California Gold Rush." History in the Headlines. Retrieved from http://www.history.com.

33. HistoryLink.org. Online encyclopedia of Washington State history. "Sisters of Providence Open Their First Seattle Hospital on Aug. 2, 1878." Essay 461 by Mildred Andrews, Dec 8, 1998. Retrieved from http://www.historylink.org/index.cfm.

34. London, J. (1906). "The Story of an Eyewitness." *Colliers' National Weekly.* Jean and Charles Schultz Information Center, Sonoma State University, Roy Tennant and Clarice Statz. Retrieved from http://www.london.sonoma.edu.

35. California Department of Parks and Recreation (1906). "Story of an Eyewitness, Jack London." California Department of Parks and Recreation. Retrieved from www.parks.ca.gov/?page_id=24206.

36. National parks. History and Culture. Klondike Gold Rush—Seattle. Retrieved from www.nps.gov/klse/historyculture/.

37. California Department of Parks and Recreation (1906). "1906

San Francisco Earthquake." California Department of Parks and Recreation. Retrieved from www.parks.ca.gov/?page_id=24204 6.

38. Fleming, S. (2011). *Grand multipare's experiences of birthing in US hospitals: A Heideggerian hermeneutic study* (doctoral dissertation). Chair: Roxanne Vandermause. Retrieved at: http://gradworks.umi.com/34/60/3460382.html

39. Bellevue Hospital Center/ NYU Langome Medical Center (2013). Retrieved from http://www.med.nyu.edu/patients-vistors/our-hospitals/bellevue-hospital-center.

40. Playfair, W.S. (1880). *A Treatise on the Science and Practice of Midwifery*. 3rd edition. Philadelphia: Henry C. Lea.

41. HistoryLink.org. Online encyclopedia of Washington State history. "Children's Orthopedic Hospital." Essays 2059 & 3363 by Mildred Andrews. Retrieved from http://www.historylink.org/index.cfm.

42. Seattle Children's Hospital. *"1907 The Beginning of Seattle Children's."* Retrieved from http://www.seattlechildrens.org/about/history. "Seattle Children's Hospital 1909 to 1915: A Proper Hospital." Retrieved from http://www.seattlechildrens.org/about/history.

43. Howe, W. (1918) *Care of the Expectant Mother* (copyright 1903). Philadelphia: F.A. Davis.

44. American Medical Association. Retrieved from http://www.ama-assn.org/ama.

45. American Osteopathic Association. Retrieved from

http://www.osteopathic.org/Pages/default.aspx.

46. American Congress of Obstetricians and Gynecologists, ACOG. Retrieved from https://www.acog.org.

47. American Academy of Pediatrics. AAP. Retrieved from https://www.aap.org.

48. Midwives' Association of Washington State. History of MAWS. Retrieved from http://www.washingtonmidwives.org/about-maws-history.html.

49. Lloyd, R. (2012) *"An Example for Us." Ellis Shipp was early Utah female physician.* Retrieved from http//www.ldschurchnews.com.

50. Utah History Encyclopedia. History of Ellis Reynolds Shipp, Utah. Retrieved from http://www.onlineutah.com/shipp_ellis_reynolds_history_02.s html.

51. Wardell, J. (1984). "Ellis Reynolds Shipp: Mother and Doctor." *The Friend.* Church of Jesus Christ, Salt Lake City, UT. Retrieved from https://www.lds.org/friend/1984/04/ellis-reynolds-shipp-mother-and-doctor?lang=eng.

52. Frontier Nursing University (2013). History. Retrieved from http://www.frontier.edu/about-frontier/school-history.

53. American College of Nurse-Midwives. ACNM. Retrieved from https://www.midwife.org.

54. American College of Nurse Midwives. "Our History." Retrieved http://www.midwife.org/our-history.

55. American Nurses Association (2013). ANA History. Retrieved from http://www.nursingworld.org/FunctionalMenuCategories/AboutANA/History.

56. AWHONN (2013). History. Retrieved from https://www.awhonn.org/awhonn/content.do;jsessionid=804D519A93CADE05A41C23097517CF1A?name=10_AboutUs/10_History.htm.

57. American Pharmacists Association. Retrieved from http://www.pharmacist.com.

58. Illinois Infant Mortality 1907-2002 (2002). Retrieved from http://www.idph.state.il.us/health/infant/intmort07-02.htm.

59. *Seattle Times*. (2001). "150 years Seattle By and By." Researched by Vince Kueter.

60. HistoryLink.org. Online encyclopedia of Washington State history. "Denny Regrade: First Phase is Completed January 6, 1899." Essay 708 by Greg Lange. Retrieved from http://www.historylink.org/index.cfm.

61. HistoryLink.org. Online encyclopedia of Washington State history. "Pioneer Square Cybertour." Essay 7055 by Walt Crowley. Retrieved from http://www.historylink.org/index.cfm.

62. HistoryLink.org. Online encyclopedia of Washington State history. "Bubonic Plague Kills a Seattle Resident on October 19, 1907." Essay 418 by Pricilla Long. Retrieved from http://www.historylink.org/index.cfm.

63.   Medline Plus (2013). Plague. Retrieved from
        http://www.nlm.nih.gov/medlineplus/ency/article/000596.htm

64.   Alexander, J.W. (2009). "History of the Medical Use of
        Silver." Surgical Infections. Vol 10(3).
        http://tse.colloidalsilverkillsviruses.com/pdf/history.pdf

65.   Navy Department Library. "The Cruise of the Great White
        Fleet-Naval History and Heritage." Retrieved from.
        www.history.navy.mil/library/online/gwf_cruise.htm

66.   HistoryLink.org. Online encyclopedia of Washington State
        history. "Great White Fleet Visits Seattle on May 23, 1908."
        Essay 3610 by David Wilma. Retrieved from
        http://www.historylink.org/index.cfm.

67.   "USN *Kansas* Hit Port." *Seattle Times* Sunday newspaper
        archives. May 31, 1908, p. 12. Text from www.Genealogy
        Bank.com.

68.   Washington State Nurses Association. "Our History."
        Retrieved from http://www.wsna.org.

69.   HistoryLink.org. Online encyclopedia of Washington State
        history. "Alaska-Yukon-Pacific Exposition (1909): Baby
        Incubator Exhibit and Café." Essay 8921 by Paula Becker.
        Retrieved from http://www.historylink.org/index.cfm.

70.   Bartley, N. (2009). "Memorable Time When Seattle Was
        'World of Wonder' 1909." *Seattle Times.* February 23, 2009.

71.   HistoryLink.org. Online encyclopedia of Washington State
        history. "Alaska-Yukon-Pacific Exposition (1909): Woman
        Suffrage." Essay 8587 by Paula Becker. Retrieved from

http://www.historylink.org/index.cfm.

72. "Political Rights Women Fail to Register." *Seattle Times*. Dec 8, 1908. Genealogybank.com

73. "Timeline of Women's Suffrage in the United States." Retrieved from http://dpsinfo.com/women/history/timeline.html.

74. HistoryLink.org. Online encyclopedia of Washington State history. "Woman Suffrage Crusade, 1848-1920." Essay 5662 by Mildred Andrews. February 26, 2004. http://www.historylink.org/index.cfm.

75. Mother Ryther.org. Mother Ryther. Retrieved from http://www.ryther.org/legacy/.

76. HistoryLink.org. Online encyclopedia of Washington State history. "Ryther, Mother Olive." Essay 546 by Mildred Andrews. Retrieved from http://www.historylink.org/index.cfm.

77. HistoryLink.org. Online encyclopedia of Washington State history. "Flu Epidemic Hits Seattle on October 3, 1918." Essay 2090 by David Wilma. Retrieved from http://www.historylink.org/index.cfm.

78. "The Great Pandemic." US Department of Health Services. Retrieved from http://www.flu.gov/pandemic/history/1918/index.html.

79. HistoryLink.org. Online encyclopedia of Washington State history. "The Flu Epidemic Hits Seattle on October 3, 1918." http://www.historylink.org/index.cfm?DisplayPage=output.cf

m&file_id=2090

80. HistoryLink.org. Online encyclopedia of Washington State history. "Flu Epidemic Hits Seattle on October 3, 1918." Essay 2090 by David Wilma. Retrieved from http://www.historylink.org/index.cfm.

81. Danklefsen, Ralph. Personal family story of his family saving another family during the flu pandemic. Told to Susan Fleming 2007.

82. "Grandfather Gets His Hand Hurt." *Seattle Times*. July 4, 1909. Genealogybank.com.

83. HistoryLink.org. Online encyclopedia of Washington State history. "Depression, The Great 1929-1939." Essay 3717 by David Wilma. Retrieved from http://www.historylink.org/index.cfm.

84. Gregory, J. (2009). "Economics and Poverty." University of Washington. The Great Depression in Washington State Project. Retrieved from https://depts.washington.edu/depress/.

Suggested Readings

Frankl, Viktor E. *Man's Search for Meaning*. Boston: Beacon Press, 2006.

Simkin, Penny. *The Birth Partner: A Complete Guide to Childbirth for Dads, Doulas, and All Other Labor Companions*. Fourth edition. Boston: Harvard Common Press, 2008.

Ulrich, Laurel Thatcher. *A Midwife's Tale: The Life of Martha Ballard, Based on Her Diary, 1785-1812*. New York: Knopf, 1990.

Worth, Jennifer, *Call the Midwife: A Memoir of Birth, Joy, and Hard Times*. New York: Penguin Books, 2012.

Selected Bibliography

Berner, Richard C. *Seattle 1900-1920: From Boomtown, Urban Turbulence, to Restoration.* Seattle: Charles Press, 1991.

Blackburn, S. (2007). *Maternal, Fetal, and Neonatal Physiology. A Clinical Perspective.* (3rd ed.). St. Louis: Saunders.

Crowley, Walt; David W. Wilma and HistoryLink staff. *Hope on the Hill: The First Century of Seattle Children's Hospital.* United States: HistoryLink and University of Washington Press, 2010.

London, M., Ladewig, P., Davidson, M., Ball, J., Bindler, R. & Cowen, K. (2014). *Maternal & Child Nursing Care.* 4th ed. Upper Saddle River, NJ: Pearson/Prentice Hall

Morgan, Lael. *Good Time Girls of the Alaska-Yukon Gold Rush: Secret History of the Far North.* Fairbanks, Alaska: Epicenter Press, 1998.

Potter, P., & Perry, A. (2013). *Fundamentals of Nursing.* 8th ed. St. Louis Missouri: Elsevier

Rooks, Judith. *Midwifery and Childbirth in America.* Philadelphia: Temple University Press, 1997.

Starr, P. (1982). *The Social Transformation of American Medicine.* New York: Basic Books.

Stein, Alan J. and Paula Becker, *Alaska-Yukon-Pacific Exposition: Washington's First World's Fair: A Timeline History.* United States: History Ink/History Link with University of Washington Press, 2009.

Wertz, Richard and Dorothy. *Lying-In: A History of Childbirth in America.* Expanded edition. New Haven: Yale University Press, 1989.

Keepers of Seattle's Remarkable History

HistoryLink.org is a free, online encyclopedia of Seattle, King County, and Washington State history. Website: historylink.org

Seattle's Museum of History & Industry (MOHAI). Website: www.mohai.org

Seattle City Municipal Archives contains historic city files, maps, and photographs. Website: www.seattle.gov/cityarchives/

The *Seattle Times* history project, "150 Years: Seattle By and By," a series published between May and November 2001 to mark the city's 150th anniversary. Website: www.seattletimes.com/news/local/seattle_history.

University of Washington Archives, including the UW Digital Historical Collection and Special Collections about the university and the Pacific Northwest. Website: www.lib.washington.edu

History House of Greater Seattle, which preserves and exhibits Seattle's diverse neighborhoods, history, and heritage. Website: www.historyhouse.org

Historic Seattle, preservers of Seattle's architectural past. Website: www.historicseattle.org

Puget Sound Maritime Historical Society, preservers of the Northwest's nautical heritage. Website: www.pugetmaritime.org

To all the individuals and families of Seattle that have contributed to keeping the magnificent history of Seattle alive.

Recommended Midwifery Sites:

An homage to midwives "being" with women, as well as to doulas and childbirth educators.

American College of Nurse-Midwives, http://www.midwife.org/

University of Washington School of Nursing Midwifery Program http://nursing.uw.edu/academic-services/degree-programs/nm/nurse-midwifery.html

Bastyr University's Seattle Midwifery School, http://www.bastyr.edu/seattle-midwifery-school-now-part-bastyr

Bloom Spokane, http://www.bloomspokane.com/

Doulas International, http://www.dona.org/mothers/

International Confederation of Midwives, http://www.midwives2014.org/

Lamaze International, http://www.lamaze.org/

Midwives Alliance, http://www.mana.org/

Midwives' Association of Washington, http://www.washingtonmidwives.org/

Midwifery Today, http://www.midwiferytoday.com/

Noteworthy Nursing and Physician Websites

I extend praise to doctors and nurses who care for expectant mothers during pregnancy and birth.

American Nurses Association, http://www.nursingworld.org/

Association of Women's Health, Obstetric and Neonatal Nurses AWHONN, https://www.awhonn.org/awhonn/

American Congress of Obstetricians and Gynecologists, http://www.acog.org/

American Academy of Pediatrics, http://www.aap.org

American Academy of Family Physicians, http://www.aafp.org

American Osteopathic Association, http://www.osteopathic.org/Pages/default.aspx

American Pharmacists Association, http://www.pharmacist.com

Washington nursing, http://www.nurse.org/wa-index.shtml

Donna Maheady's resources for nurses with disabilities, http://www.exceptionalnurse.com/

Phone app sites:

A special thanks to Dr. Aron Schuftan and Dr. Jan Rydfors for listening to today's technologically capable childbearing women. Two highly respected OBGYNs created this mom/baby/doctor friendly app and website.

~Pregnancy Companion: http://www.pregnancycompanionapp.com/

~ILamaze Girl free breathing app:
https://itunes.apple.com/us/app/ilamaze-girl-free/id468593562?mt=8
~March of Dimes app My 9 Months:
https://itunes.apple.com/us/app/my-9-months/id528623198?mt=8

Old West Slang Dictionary
(from www.legendsofamerica.com/we-slang-s.htm)

Backdoor trots = Diarrhea

Bad egg = A bad person

Big pasture = penitentiary

Boozy = intoxicated

Calico queen = prostitute

Cut and Run = to be off

Ditty = a whatcha-ma-call-it

Eagle = a ten-dollar coin

Firewater = liquor

French pox = syphilis

Foundlings = orphans

Grass Widow = a divorcee

Hitched = married

Left-handed wife = mistress

Lookin' to die = seriously ill

Packin' iron = carrying a gun

Sawbones = a surgeon

Texas cakewalk = a hanging

Please find us on **www.seattlepioneermidwife.com** for current events, book signings and local bookstores.

CPSIA information can be obtained at www.ICGtesting.com
Printed in the USA
LVOW12s2132120514

385524LV00013B/357/P